LARGE PRINT
CROSSWORDS

Publications International, Ltd.

Let's get social!

@Publications_International

@PublicationsInternational

@BrainGames.TM

www.pilbooks.com

DECLUTTER AND UNWIND

We all have thoughts and worries that swirl through our heads each and every day. Did I remember to close the garage door? Did I turn on the alarm? Hopefully, you can still find time to declutter your mind and perhaps even unwind. *Brain Games® Large Print Crosswords* is an excellent way to decompress and relax.

With more than 80 large print crossword puzzles designed to be easy on the eyes, *Brain Games® Large Print Crosswords* tests your knowledge on a range of subjects.

Each puzzle is spread out across two pages making both grids and clues easier to read. If you find yourself stuck, the answers are conveniently located at the back of the book.

Do you have what it takes to scale the mountain of knowledge and solve this assortment of puzzles? We hope so, and, wish you good luck.

HODGEPODGE

ACROSS

5. Cause of odd weather
7. Bound by routine
9. "Jeopardy!" emcee, e.g.
10. The nitty-gritty
14. Amazing to behold
16. Supposed face in the sky
19. For nothing
20. Catch fire

DOWN

1. Very thin layer
2. John of "Dynasty"
3. "Flintstones" pet
4. Floats ashore
6. Brewpub beverages
8. Bear among the stars
11. Nicollette of "Desperate Housewives"
12. Tailor's objective
13. Loosen, as a lace
15. Agricultural building
17. Panzer division vehicle
18. "You gotta be kidding!"

ANSWERS ON PAGE 172

MEDLEY

ACROSS

1. Crunchy snack
8. Cal. barrio locale
9. Big wheel
11. Labor leader played by Nicholson
12. Birmingham resource
13. Moses parted it
15. Echo effect
18. Keep going
20. Brain covering
22. Opposite of "o'er"
23. Becomes, at last
24. Radar gun sites

DOWN

2. 9-to-5 routine
3. B vitamin
4. Buzzwords, collectively
5. "Road" movies star
6. Bouncing toy
7. Baby cow
10. Leg revealing garment
14. Delivery time
16. Got less intense
17. Not sitting idle
19. TV listing
21. "Negatory"

ANSWERS ON PAGE 172

GRAB BAG

ACROSS

7. It's usually called a strike
8. Chopping tools
9. First installment
10. Badges with handles
12. Adult
14. Bounding gait
16. Dresden dweller
17. Like good kids
19. Turnblad in "Hairspray"
20. Cold War competition

DOWN

1. "I like it!"
2. Crab delicacy
3. Argentine grassland
4. Buffy, to vampires
5. Dangerous carnivore
6. Bartender's twist
11. Air raid ender
13. One beyond hope
15. Craft commanded by JFK
16. Advance from third
17. Group consent phrase
18. Change from time to time

ANSWERS ON PAGE 172

A BIT OF WORDPLAY

ACROSS

1. "Star Wars" pilot
5. Bus station
8. Musical staff symbol
9. Sirius (or Lassie?)
10. Extremely simple
13. Became waterless
14. Christie of whodunits
17. Get suspicious
21. Get some air
22. End of the Pacific war
23. Big name in copiers
24. Destroyers, in Navy lingo

DOWN

1. Bigger than big
2. "Antony and Cleopatra" river
3. 2019, 2021, or 2023, with respect to elections
4. Somewhat passé
5. Fixed belief
6. Miniature golf, informally
7. Like some light bulbs
11. Media section
12. Canal site
15. Exact revenge
16. High-priority
18. House paint ingredient
19. "Aha moment" cause
20. "Y" facilities

ANSWERS ON PAGE 172

COMMON PHRASES

ACROSS

5. Receive a promotion
7. Was able to endure
8. Dorm room light
9. Midnight fridge visit
10. How destitute people may live
12. Calling the shots
14. Basic teachings
15. Water conduit
17. Be cruel to
18. 1994 Johnny Depp title role

DOWN

1. Jacob's eleventh son
2. Watered down
3. Circumvent
4. Come to an end
6. Obey the rules
7. Tailor's tool
11. Absolutely no one
12. Economical way to buy
13. Account for holding
16. Break of day

ANSWERS ON PAGE 173

AN OCULAR PUZZLE

ACROSS

7. "As we speak..."
9. Athlete's best effort
10. Lovely to look on
11. "S.N.L." alum Cheri
13. Offs, gangster-style
16. "Deal with it!"
17. Artillery discharge
18. They help you see
21. Cry of despair
22. Cheer on

DOWN

1. "OK, I'm starting now..."
2. A minor and others
3. Quick as a wink
4. Bake sale item
5. Raggedy Ann, for one
6. Own (up)
8. Appliance needed for a hot bath
12. Delighting in
14. Greyhound station, e.g.
15. Suit bottom
18. Armed forces VIP
19. "Beg your pardon..."
20. Umpire's call

ANSWERS ON PAGE 173

POTPOURRI

ACROSS

1. Response to an interruption
6. Clump of feathers
8. "No need to dress up"
9. "All sales final"
10. Levies on booze and such
11. Settler transportation of the Old West
15. Inaccurately designated
18. Academic challenge
19. Play miniature golf?
20. Baylor mascot
21. Craft of espionage

DOWN

2. Metal cutter
3. Domesticates
4. Doesn't fold, in poker
5. Assess in a fitting room
6. Big wave
7. Gift getter's question
12. Pursue
13. Soviet military force
14. Be a sub
16. Coming in handy
17. Angler's assortment
18. Of the same value

ANSWERS ON PAGE 173

PHRASE ASSORTMENT

ACROSS

1. Dude ranch visitor
7. Arm of the Atlantic
8. Tease relentlessly
9. Inner circle member
10. Not quite with it
11. Basketball strategy
14. Nonstandard auto feature
16. Have no doubt
18. Apple or mountain
19. Personification of America
20. Classic Christmas carol

DOWN

1. Atoll material
2. Anti-nuke action
3. Full of back talk
4. Right away
5. "M*A*S*H" setting
6. House of Lancaster emblem
11. Homemade weapons
12. Ladies' man
13. Savings for later in life
15. "Consider it done!"
16. Breakfast meat
17. Tribute with good-natured ribbing

ANSWERS ON PAGE 173

ACROSS

6. Shared, like a characteristic
8. Diplomatic agreement
9. "I'd rather not"
10. Do without food
11. Paycheck booster
14. Hiking venues
15. Like some unnatural blondes
17. Like Cinderella's stepsisters
19. Damaging gossip
20. Precisely as scheduled

DOWN

1. "Diana" singer Paul
2. Travels with a wagon train, e.g.
3. Without hesitation
4. English, in billiards
5. Contemptuous
7. Selfish people
12. "Don't let that bother you"
13. Old-style calculating machines
16. "It was somebody else!"
18. Pointer's word

ANSWERS ON PAGE 174

FIGURATIVE PLACES

ACROSS

1. Be a guest of
8. Veteran sailors
9. Hired muscle
10. "Y.M.C.A." singers
11. Accept a proposal
13. Regained consciousness
17. Easy task
20. "Not gonna do it!"
21. Things may disappear here
22. Big dog

DOWN

1. Compared with
2. Head and shoulders cover
3. "Missed your chance!"
4. Like a good drill team
5. "I'll take a card"
6. Kid's dirty "dessert"
7. "Duly noted"
12. Brick road color
14. Endured humiliation
15. Symbol of might
16. Venus de Milo, for one
17. Prodigy, in slang
18. Suitcase label
19. Arabian gulf

ANSWERS ON PAGE 174

BEST TIME FOR A PARTY

ACROSS

1. One, of, the, errors, here
8. Groom's last hurrah
9. Accepted eagerly
10. First part of a process
11. Hemingway or Tubb
13. Some plasterwork
17. Circulatory conduit
19. Billiard ball bounce
20. Inferred okay
21. Very soon

DOWN

1. Cost of a taxi
2. Personified detergent
3. Lots, as of trouble
4. Build a fire under
5. Safety restraint
6. Title villain of a James Bond flick
7. What Orpheus strummed
12. Infatuated with
14. Desert procession
15. Electrician's rule
16. "Enough already!"
17. A bit pretentious
18. The Indy 500 drivers, for one
19. Circular storage medium

ANSWERS ON PAGE 174

WRITTEN AND SPOKEN

ACROSS

7. Inbox clutter
8. "Let's do this thing!"
9. Type of radio enthusiast
10. Be extremely frugal
12. "It was a dark and ___ night..."
14. Develop
16. Hunting lures
17. Parting words
20. Sonnet source
21. "Stop," for one

DOWN

1. Overdo the sentiment
2. Dieter's drink
3. Intensify
4. Dust jacket comments
5. Droop in the heat
6. Game with sets and runs
11. Slow cooker
13. Obviously
15. Gripping tool
16. Perform perfectly
18. Start of a piercing rebuke?
19. Above the strike zone

ANSWERS ON PAGE 174

BIRDS AND FLOWERS

ACROSS

1. Symbols of America
7. "To sum up..."
8. Tony or Obie
10. First light
13. Fried chicken choice
14. Alluring beachwear
17. Indignant reply
21. Opera house, with "la"
22. Get to the bottom of
23. Comfortable situation

DOWN

1. Control tower image
2. Filled with greenery
3. Display of self-importance
4. Blow a gasket
5. A sister of Calliope
6. Boo-boo protector
9. Wry humor
11. Dirty looks
12. First garment material
15. By mistake
16. Cares for
18. Bowled over
19. Trunk growth
20. Singer Redding

ANSWERS ON PAGE 175

ACROSS

1. Large depression for water
5. Bouillon bits
8. "Goodbye, Pierre"
9. Male protagonist
10. Salon employee
12. Benedictine head
14. Aisle worker
16. They come on when you stop
19. Generic images
20. "Add to cart" business
21. Unifying idea
22. Creator of the Grinch

DOWN

1. Goof off
2. Richards of the Stones
3. Like someone tired of talking
4. Collection of abridged works
5. Wait
6. Standout in a small pond
7. Con artists
11. Feline with a mottled coat
13. Bad way to get beat
15. Left at the altar
17. Noted performing whale
18. "Sound of Music" setting

ANSWERS ON PAGE 175

RED, WHITE, BLUE

ACROSS

1. Come to a standstill
6. Spider homes
8. Got hot under the collar
9. Grade better than a C
10. Florida vacation site
12. Acupuncture item
13. Up the creek
14. World Cup bouncer
17. "Get real!"
18. Key with one sharp
19. Yearning
20. At large

DOWN

2. Lions or Tigers or Bears
3. Common scam
4. "What's likely is…"
5. One of the United Arab Emirates
6. Bicolor wheel
7. Low-risk investment
11. Moment of attack
13. "Success!"
15. Be as much as
16. Brown bubbly beverage

ANSWERS ON PAGE 175

KNOWLEDGE IS POWER

ACROSS

1. Fizzy drink with flavored syrup
6. Like press-on fingernails
8. Gov't investments
9. Refused
10. "Could be worse"
11. Currently plentiful
12. Excited like Miss Piggy?
16. 2006 movie of Helen Mirren
18. Dock area
19. Before it's too late
20. One and all, among guys
21. Avian bill
22. Flavor detector

DOWN

2. Seek revenge against
3. Hurt deeply
4. Subsequent
5. Covers up
6. On the level
7. More or less
13. Fires up
14. Loose coins
15. Coleridge setting
17. Apply with intensity

ANSWERS ON PAGE 175

A TASTY PUZZLE

ACROSS

6. Idiot box
8. Bring crashing down
9. Money for buying Oreos?
10. Crossed through
12. Got right
13. Avid supporter
15. Way to address someone specifically
16. Picnic side dish
18. "It's ___ vu all over again!"
19. Dirty dealing

DOWN

1. Anjou alternative
2. Charmingly retro
3. Like some collisions
4. Inadvertently revealing remark
5. Headlight setting
7. Vent to relieve tension
11. Homer or Dante
14. Get word to
15. Smash to bits
17. "Saving Private Ryan" event

ANSWERS ON PAGE 176

ACROSS

7. California racetrack
8. Comes up
9. Try something out
10. Queens stadium name
12. Loyal politician
14. Prime minister of Queen Victoria's reign
16. Emma Stone's "___ Land"
17. Last-ditch play
20. Exit the system
21. Atlantic archipelago

DOWN

1. Arctic Sea floater
2. Cheap flick
3. Peach cobbler, for example
4. "Til next time!"
5. "A ___ Fortress Is Our God"
6. Where steins are raised
11. Crow's-nest cry
13. Something to save for
15. Deodorant on a ball
16. Apply pressure to
18. Volvo or VW
19. Get angrier and angrier

ANSWERS ON PAGE 176

Q MARKS THE SPOT

ACROSS

1. White orb with no number
5. Artist's theme
8. Singer LaBelle
9. Marshmallow sandwich
10. Hard labor spot
11. Homeless child
13. New Orleans district
15. Cafe au ___
17. Captain Hook's foe
20. "Imagine that!"
21. One score after deuce
22. "Over There" soldiers
23. Bureaucratic nonsense

DOWN

1. Manages somehow
2. Getty of "The Golden Girls"
3. More than one can handle
4. Tool for making tart fruit juice
5. Kitty's comment
6. Aggressive sort
7. Sympathize with
12. King, queen or jack
13. One left holding the bag
14. Dessert pudding
16. Explanatory intro
18. "Find somebody else!"
19. In this way

ANSWERS ON PAGE 176

FUN AND GAMES

ACROSS

1. Boxer's weak spot
5. Belt hole makers
8. Pronoun of the queen
9. Art gallery
10. Carried, as a gun
11. Get a sense of
12. "Big Easy" festival
15. Headlight setting
16. Start of a series
18. Water threesome
19. Nobody at all
20. Kind of rock music
21. Intimidate

DOWN

1. Do the twist
2. At this point
3. Spinach, lettuce, etc.
4. Boss in a red suit
6. Small parts
7. Performed a ballad for
9. Example of dirty politics
12. Decimate, as an army
13. "Li'l Abner" cartoonist
14. Achieve success
17. 8×10, for one

ANSWERS ON PAGE 176

IT'S IN THE AIR

ACROSS

7. Cart away
9. 18, generally
10. Godiva choice
11. Clever people
12. Attack from above
15. Mike, to Archie Bunker
16. Look at
19. How many fall in love
21. Reformer Ralph
22. Way up the slope

DOWN

1. Follow covertly
2. Way to prepare potatoes
3. Express, as an opinion
4. Become a sailor
5. Gulf of California peninsula
6. Amp effect
8. Sunshine State vacation area
13. Dressing component
14. Part of the team
15. Egyptian tourist attraction
17. Aware of
18. Arab chief
20. Nurse's assistant

ANSWERS ON PAGE 177

A VACATION FROM CLEANING

ACROSS

7. Ancient Chinese text
8. Add water to
9. It really sucks
11. Compare the costs of
13. Have too much sun, perhaps
15. All shook up
17. Absolutely detest
18. Common policy on vacation time
20. Stop, as a leak
21. Former justice Antonin

DOWN

1. Venom source
2. All the rage
3. Like harmonious bands
4. Musical deficiency
5. Directly up, on a map
6. Become tattered
10. French wine region
12. Where to nip it
14. Pub hurlers
16. Kind of test
17. Without further ado
18. Ballpark figures
19. Aquatic zappers

ANSWERS ON PAGE 177

MELANGE

ACROSS

1. Place for a plug
7. Become sick
8. "Glee" extra
10. Like Mayberry
11. Don't press your luck
12. Camper's shelter
14. "As a matter of fact, I do"
17. Canine competition
19. Giving approval to
21. Wheels with a meter
22. Joins the rank and file
23. Wisely invested funds

DOWN

1. Chute by the pool
2. Los Angeles athlete
3. "Start talking!"
4. Without freaking out
5. Erode
6. Slipped away, as time
9. United Press International, for one
13. Blanket or dog
15. Gang member
16. Plead to get
18. Accepted rule
20. "Hedda Gabler" playwright Henrik

ANSWERS ON PAGE 177

THREE FROM ABC

ACROSS

1. Early computer language for business
6. Greedy sort
11. Daggers, in footnotes
12. From the beginning, in Latin
13. Action-adventure series starring Lynda Carter as Diana Prince
15. Health-food phrase
16. "To a Skylark," e.g.
17. Ending for lamp or harp
18. Pulitzer biographer Leon
19. Sitcom starring Jane Levy as Tessa Altman
23. Scott Turow book about Harvard Law School
24. Three-match link
25. Summer hrs. in Colorado
26. Lumberjacks
30. Comedy-drama with William Shatner as Denny Crane
32. First month in Mexico
33. Muse of love poetry
34. California's Point ___ National Seashore
35. Sight or taste, e.g

DOWN

1. Monk's head covering
2. Mellow woodwind
3. Affleck and Kingsley
4. King Cole was a merry one
5. Try to protect, in a way
6. Believed, to Tweety
7. Blood-type letters
8. ___ dragon (largest living lizard)
9. One who slips away
10. Star of the 1960s series "Tarzan"
14. Capital of Myanmar (Burma)
18. Knickknack furniture
19. Like a requiem
20. How some knots come
21. Fashion designer Johnson

22. Geometry measurements
26. "Gentlemen Prefer Blondes" author Anita
27. Alaska's first governor William A. ___
28. Pied Piper followers
29. Gin-flavoring fruit
31. One less than quattro

1	2	3	4	5		6	7	8	9	10
11						12				
13				14						
15								16		
			17				18			
19	20	21				22				
23					24					
25				26				27	28	29
30			31							
32						33				
34						35				

ANSWERS ON PAGE 177

ACROSS THE BOARD

ACROSS

1. Board game about personal milestones
5. Dispatches, as a fly
10. First Oscar winner Jannings
11. Old Roman robes
12. Seas, to Napoleon
13. Spar verbally
14. Code-breaking board game for two players
16. Dramatist Chekhov
17. UFO crew
18. Where Fargo is: abbr.
21. AT&T or Comcast, online-wise: abbr.
24. Lightweight cottons
28. Board game of bluffing and trivia
31. Delicacy in a shell
32. "One can only ___ much"
33. Old lab gas burners
34. Cube inventor Rubik
35. House of Lords member
36. Board game of strategy and diplomacy

DOWN

1. Premise of a syllogism
2. "Let me explain..."
3. Blue-ribbon position
4. Howard of baseball fame
5. Marquee name
6. Early bird's prize
7. Farm school student
8. Talk smack to
9. Bird-feeder fill
15. Conclude
19. Earth Day mo.
20. One pulling your leg
21. "A Doll's House" author
22. ___ Domingo (Caribbean capital)
23. Backup option
25. New Zealand native
26. NBA and PGA
27. Closed a deal, in a way
29. Obsolete phone feature
30. "If all ___ fails..."

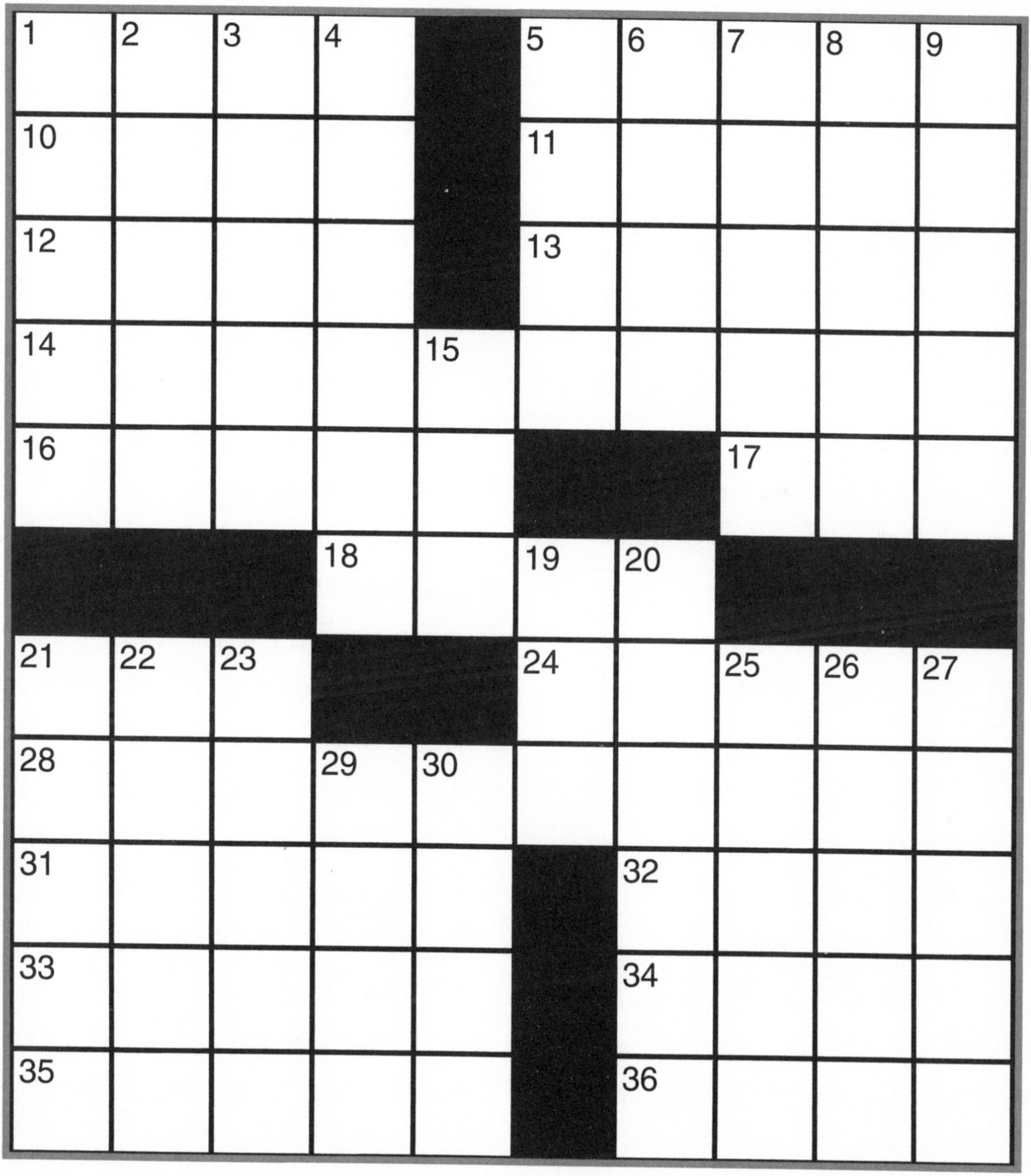

ANSWERS ON PAGE 178

ALL IN GOOD TIME

ACROSS

1. With 35-Across, worn timepiece
6. British strollers
11. Prefix for "sun"
12. Apt to cause the willies
13. Cupcake topper
14. Pasta like ziti
15. Chirpy timepiece on the wall
17. Bit of a chuckle
18. Double daggers, in printing
19. Judge played by Stallone
21. Extinguish
24. Big inits. in bowling
27. Ship's timepiece, e.g.
30. Literature Nobelist Pirandello
31. Change "captain" to "cap'n," e.g.
32. "You ___ big trouble!"
33. Dragon with Kukla and Fran
34. Air Force installations
35. See 1-Across

DOWN

1. "This one? Or this one?"
2. Prompt again, as an actor
3. Peter ___ Tchaikovsky
4. Kitchen essential
5. Food takeout order
6. Zantac rival
7. Spun around
8. Works by New Yorker cartoonist Peter
9. Chop finely
10. Goes on a quest
16. "___ a Nightingale" (Keats poem)
19. Young TV doc Howser
20. Encounters
21. High-tech classroom
22. Nichelle Nichols's role on "Star Trek"
23. Makes an effort
24. Like the Leaning Tower
25. Battlefield doc

26. FBI chief after Sessions 29. "Enchanted" film girl
28. Kitty's cry

1	2	3	4	5		6	7	8	9	10
11						12				
13						14				
15					16					
17					18					
			19	20						
21	22	23						24	25	26
27						28	29			
30						31				
32						33				
34						35				

 ANSWERS ON PAGE 178

AT THE DROP OF A HAT

ACROSS
1. De Gaulle trademark hat
5. Alda or Ladd
9. Presley's middle name
10. "The Lord of the Rings," e.g.
11. Broccoli ___ (salad green)
12. Military inst.
13. Lincoln's hat type
15. Played, as a cat with a mouse
16. Poetic "always"
17. Bad toupee
19. Feeling peaked
22. Kinkajou cousin
26. Rain hat à la Gorton's fisherman
28. It goes in the pot
29. ___-Flush (bathroom cleaner)
30. Geological periods
31. More than annoys
32. Price-tag info
33. Helmet type for a safari leader

DOWN
1. Land formation known for its caves
2. Muse of poetry
3. New Orleans sandwich, informally
4. "The very thought!"
5. "Pronto!" initials
6. "Alice in Wonderland" sister
7. Obviously amazed
8. Consumer activist Ralph
14. Draw out
18. Scuttlebutt
19. Asimov of sci-fi
20. Start and end of "O Sole Mio"
21. Minstrels' instruments
23. "Pong" company
24. Church principle
25. Dublin denizens
27. Greeley's preferred direction

Crossword grid with numbered cells:

1	2	3	4	■	5	6	7	8
9				■	10			
11				■	12			
13				14				
15					■	16		
■	■	■	17		18	■	■	■
19	20	21	■	22		23	24	25
26			27					
28				■	29			
30				■	31			
32				■	33			

57

AT THE TRATTORIA

ACROSS

1. Pub. staffers
4. Army posts
9. Long narrow inlet
10. About 70 percent of Earth's surface
11. Trattoria starter
13. Come across as
14. Original Dungeons & Dragons co.
15. Come across as
18. Trattoria entree
21. Enter carefully
22. French friend
23. Spanish bar tidbit
27. Trattoria entree go-with
30. Aquarium problem
31. Certain MIT grads
32. Ruth's mother-in-law
33. Cheshire grinner

DOWN

1. Chapters in history
2. Chow down, more formally
3. Appease, as hunger
4. Charlie Parker's genre
5. Here, in Acapulco
6. Group of six singers
7. Bothers persistently
8. "Edda" author ___ Sturluson
12. PR firm's concern
16. Greek F
17. Prefix meaning "five"
18. Male sailor
19. Actress ___ Sue Martin
20. Pungent Italian cheese
24. Baldwin who was Jack Ryan
25. Legal bargain
26. Administrative aide: abbr.
28. Bagpiper's cap
29. "___ Mir Bist Du Schoen": 1937 hit

ANSWERS ON PAGE 178

BEST OF FRENEMIES

ACROSS

1. Anthony and Chagall
6. Excuse from a suspect
11. Joyce's Leopold
12. Big name in briefs
13. The Hulk's nemesis
15. Store freebies
16. Dynamite letters
17. To the max, for short
18. Puente known as "The Mambo King"
19. Peter Pan's antagonist
23. "He makes no friend who never made ___" (Tennyson)
24. Last of 26
25. NCO rank
26. Gives the appearance of
30. Iron Man's adversary
32. Actresses Turner and Wood
33. Grassy plain of South America
34. ___ nous (between us)
35. "It's nobody ___ business"

DOWN

1. CEO degrees
2. Jessica of "Fantastic Four"
3. Motel vacancy
4. Do a math job
5. "___'s Sense of Snow" (Peter Hoeg novel)
6. Exclamations of discovery
7. Back muscle, for short
8. Ab ___ (from the beginning)
9. Understand now, as someone's tricks
10. Falls short of being acceptable
14. Regular on the Web
18. Teen hangout
19. Home for a king
20. Knitted blanket
21. Packing a punch
22. Compass pointer
26. Business-letter encl.
27. Spanish ladies, for short
28. Fork tooth

29. Yoko's family

31. Damage superficially

1	2	3	4	5	■	6	7	8	9	10
11					■	12				
13					14					
15							■	16		
■	■	■	17			■	18			
19	20	21				22				
23				■	24			■	■	■
25			■	26				27	28	29
30			31							
32					■	33				
34					■	35				

ANSWERS ON PAGE 179

BODY TALK

ACROSS

1. One of a "Mikado" trio
5. "I'm glad I met ya" company
10. Salinger story girl
11. Red hog breed
12. Hitchhike
14. Flower part
15. Elevator giant
16. Minor quibble
18. French for "here"
19. Kukla or Ollie, e.g.
23. Freud's "I"
24. ___-mo (replay feature)
25. Easy tennis shots
27. Sacro- ending
31. Protection for a boxer
33. To be, in Madrid
34. Deposed Russian ruler
35. Finals and midterms
36. To be, in Paris

DOWN

1. "Amazin'" Big Apple team
2. Court legend Arthur
3. "You don't need to wake me"
4. Economics 101 topic
5. Org. concerned with tooth care
6. Currency in Germany
7. Bottom sirloin cut of beef
8. "Not happening!"
9. Scores 100 on a test
13. Radar screen dots
17. Netherlands flower
19. Football headgear
20. Words after "loose as" or "silly as"
21. "I don't want any excuses!"
22. Well-mannered
26. ASAP relative
28. Superlative ending for trick or stick
29. Budget Rent ___
30. Parrot's beak part
32. Four-baggers, in MLB

ANSWERS ON PAGE 179

BYE NOW!

ACROSS

1. Farewell, in old Rome
5. Farewell, in France
10. On the fringes, in a way
12. Dud from Detroit
13. Farewell, in Napoli
15. Cow, to a gaucho
16. Engineering grads
17. Itchy swamp shrub, poison ___ (var.)
20. Like rattan
21. Faulkner's "Requiem for ___"
22. Papal capes
24. The Atlanta Braves' div.
25. Bar brew
26. Farewell, in Moscow
31. "Me too"
32. Went out with
33. Farewell, in Cancun
34. Farewell, in Florence

DOWN

1. Important part of USIA
2. Prefix for "ear" or "gold"
3. Env. contents, possibly
4. Armenia's capital, old-style
5. "M*A*S*H" actor Alan
6. Actress Sandra or Ruby
7. 2001 #1 hit for Jennifer Lopez
8. Epoch of modern birds and mammals
9. Computer company with the slogan "Imagine it. Done."
11. Fire drill activity, briefly
14. Bounced off the walls
17. New Mexico's ___ Mountains
18. Do stevedore work
19. Granola cousin
20. Carson's swami
23. Enjoy a book
25. "About the Author" pieces
27. Brandy bottle letters
28. "Lord, is ___?": Matthew
29. Approving vote
30. Fussy excitement

ANSWERS ON PAGE 179

DOWNWARD DOG

ACROSS

1. Senior NCO
5. Kitchen appliances
11. Architect Saarinen
12. Become obvious
13. Pub drinks
14. Tried to rip open
15. Preschool program
17. Commercial spots
18. Largest flatfish
20. ___-Caps (movie candy)
22. Like Dumbledore and Santa Claus
25. Mid-16th-century pope
27. Restrain, as breath
28. Word for 3-, 5-, and 8-Down
29. Colonial insects
30. No ifs, ___ buts
31. New, in Nuremberg

DOWN

1. Anthropologist Margaret
2. Ward of "Gone Girl"
3. Swift dog
4. Opera about an opera singer
5. Golden or Labrador
6. One-celled swimmer
7. Suffix for part or vint
8. Scooby-Doo, for one
9. "Heavens to Betsy!"
10. Film locations
16. White elephant, e.g.
19. Citified
20. Animal protection org.
21. Bread served with Indian dishes
23. Caesar's question to Brutus

24. Not those, in Brooklynese   **26.** Sue Grafton's "___ For Lawless"

1	2	3	4	■	5	6	7	8	9	10
11				■	12					
13				■	14					
15				16			■	17		
■	■	18					19		■	■
20	21		■	22					23	24
25			26			■	27			
28						■	29			
30						■	31			

DUBIOUS DEFINITIONS

ACROSS

1. Short profile
4. Civil rights grp. since 1909
9. Incoming flight: abbr.
10. Canadian physician Sir William ___
11. Unwrite, as a symphony?
13. He sold out to Jacob
14. Beret cousin
15. Cassiterite or stannite
18. Took off one's Jockey shorts?
21. Take into custody
22. Peeples or Vardalos
23. Spanish hors d'oeuvre
27. Taking back the food?
30. Big name in printers
31. Casino cube
32. Like a starfish
33. T or F, on exams

DOWN

1. Said, as farewell
2. Causes wrath
3. "Free Willy" animal
4. ___ de plume (pen name)
5. Egyptian serpent
6. Many
7. Lucrezia Borgia's brother
8. Aspiring doc's program
12. Beyond unconventional
16. Sue Grafton's "___ for Innocent"
17. Hulu or Ustream, e.g.
18. Get one's ___ up: get angry
19. City down the shore from Buffalo, N.Y.
20. Like trumpet music
24. Operatic slave girl
25. Nabokov's title professor
26. Gets on in years
28. Fair-hiring inits.
29. Three-min. period, in the ring

FAIR SHARES?

ACROSS

1. Fourth Estate
6. ___ Na Na ("Grease" group)
9. Like some Coast Guard rescues
11. Arctic area: abbr.
12. Spouse, jokingly
14. Bar orders
15. Lily with arrow-shaped leaves
16. Less difficult
17. Game division
21. On a "What's Hot" list
22. Mystery writer Gardner et al.
23. Churchill prop
27. Start some origami, perhaps
29. Angelico or Diavolo
30. Sun Tzu's "___ of War"
31. Mt. Carmel locale
32. Fast horses

DOWN

1. Onetime sunblock agent
2. Cambodian coin
3. Art Deco painter
4. Booming jets of old
5. Call at poker
6. Supreme Court conservative
7. Scholar who wrote "If not now, when?"
8. Sandy sounds
10. In literature, a peaceful place
13. Corned beef dish
16. Finishes, as a relationship
17. Graf on the court
18. Blunders
19. Wine locale, often
20. Like a line, briefly
23. She had a show with Sonny
24. Tiny battery size
25. Strike-monitoring org.
26. Immature newts
28. New Deal home loan gp.

GRABBING SOME ZS

ACROSS

1. Steel beam with two right-angled bends
5. Cameron of "Charlie's Angels"
9. "Paper Lion" star Alan
10. "Judith" composer
11. Cheesy takeout orders
13. Bad guy's look
14. Bygone fast jet, briefly
15. Affront, in street slang
17. The whole amount
20. Immortal coach Amos Alonzo ___
24. Onetime inlet of the North Sea
26. Pay ___ mind
27. Switzerland's longest river
28. Great enthusiasm
29. Santa ___ Valley, California ("Sideways" setting)

DOWN

1. Cooks in a microwave
2. Light Russian pancake
3. Axe relative
4. Bulldozed
5. Fish by dropping bait lightly
6. Greek goddess of the rainbow
7. Donkeys, in Paris
8. Citrusy garnish
12. First word to a new knight, perhaps
16. Wander off
17. Comedian Ansari

18. Guitar's ancestor

19. Filmdom's Wertmuller

21. Muslim call to prayer

22. "Chicago" actor Richard

23. "Sheesh!"

25. U.S. currency unit: abbr.

1	2	3	4		5	6	7	8
9					10			
11				12				
13						14		
			15		16			
17	18	19		20		21	22	23
24			25					
26					27			
28					29			

ANSWERS ON PAGE 180

GRIPES OF WRATH

ACROSS

1. Prepare, as for action
5. Kidded
10. Japanese golf great ___ Aoki
11. ___-trump (low bridge bid)
12. Prefix with "type"
13. Like creaks at midnight
14. Puzzle video game where you take out pigs
16. "___ vous plait" (French "please")
17. Ending for real or surreal
18. Govt. auditing agency
21. Word of negation
23. They're uttered in high dudgeon
28. Album's first half
29. "___ penny, pick it up..."
30. Knoxville campus
31. Med-school subj.
32. Pampers maker, informally
33. Days of ___ (olden times)

DOWN

1. "Monster" that's a lizard
2. Hasn't left
3. Pushed a doorbell
4. House portals
5. John Q. Public's pal
6. "Dedicated to the ___ Love" (Shirelles hit)
7. Olympic gymnast Strug
8. Writers Bagnold and Blyton
9. "That thou ___, do quickly" (St. John)
15. Symbol of contrasting principles
18. Fill the tank
19. Bryant or Loos
20. Funny poet Nash
22. That is ___ (in other words)
24. Rip roughly
25. City north of Lake Tahoe
26. Start of many a letter
27. Fill to full

1
2
3
4
5
6
7
8
9
10
11
12
13
14
15
16
17
18
19
20
21
22
23
24
25
26
27
28
29
30
31
32
33

ANSWERS ON PAGE 180

HERE AND THERE

ACROSS

1. Father, in Spain
6. Quick bites in Spain
11. Sun blocker?
12. Massey of "Frankenstein Meets the Wolf Man"
13. "Conjure up the following scenario in your mind"
15. Ave. crossers, often
16. Coral formations
17. Garage band's samples
19. Conditional release
22. Audiophile's stack
25. "Well, what do you know!"
28. Basic belief
29. Pepys's legacy
30. Licorice-like flavoring
31. Building wing

DOWN

1. HMO doctor designations
2. Disembarked
3. Medical pros
4. Beaten path
5. Academic e-mail suffix
6. Connect with a rope
7. Certain singing voices
8. Science fiction author Frederik
9. Blue dye
10. Sauciness
14. Asian soup noodles
17. Former Venetian magistrates
18. The in-crowd
19. Bread for a gyro
20. Grace closing
21. Maharaja's mate

22. Charlie the sleuth

23. Be intrepid

24. River of the underworld

26. Author LeShan

27. Sardine can material

ANSWERS ON PAGE 181

HIGH TIME

ACROSS

1. Awfully high, as a price
6. Enclosed, as an estate
11. Cute Aussie "bear"
12. Chilean pianist Claudio
13. Where a dreamer's head is?
15. Spanish ayes
16. Bird's refuge
17. Hesitant sounds
19. Boat backs
23. Spiny, treelike cactus
28. Soaring
30. Bored feeling
31. Dog-walker's need
32. Theatrical platform
33. Towering

DOWN

1. Downhill gliders
2. "Beloved" novelist Morrison
3. Chows down
4. For grades 1–12, briefly
5. Bel ___ (soft cheese)
6. Square dance lass
7. Middle name at Graceland
8. Actual and factual
9. Actor George of "MacGyver"
10. Do a household chore
14. About, before a date
18. Pitchman's decoy
19. Home of Iowa State Cyclones
20. Courier or Helvetica
21. Fish in a casserole
22. Cozy

24. ___ cat (street game)
25. Bread buy
26. Passionate desire

27. Like a fireplace floor
29. Even score

1	2	3	4	5		6	7	8	9	10
11						12				
13				14						
15							16			
				17		18				
19	20	21	22		23		24	25	26	27
28			29							
30						31				
32						33				

ANSWERS ON PAGE 181

INSIDE STORY

ACROSS

1. Act like a hot dog?
5. Diplomat's asset
9. "Unattractive" fruit
10. Hindu mystic
11. "Take another shot" at a saga inside?
13. Sarcastic laugh
14. Corp. swallowed by Verizon
15. "Messenger" molecule
16. Suffix with super
17. Portrayals of an epic story inside?
21. Boy in "The Phantom Menace"
22. Cruise or Hanks
23. TV's "can cook" chef Martin
24. "You can stop explaining now"
28. Wisenheimers with a tale inside?
30. Old name for hopscotch
31. Olivia of "The Wonder Years"
32. Smell ___ (suspect a trick)
33. Help for the needy

DOWN

1. Actor Willard of "The Color Purple"
2. Cancun water
3. Dodger or Giant, for short
4. Yom Kippur's Hebrew month
5. Cry before "You're it!"
6. How "Moon River" is played
7. Rock-clinging mollusk
8. Piano adjusters
10. Site of a major American victory in the Revolutionary War
12. Holiness
17. Pampering place
18. Romantically charm
19. Target at the fiesta
20. Marcos who collected shoes

25. Blue-green hue
26. Long-range weapon, briefly
27. General ___ chicken (Chinese menu item)
29. They're right in front of U

1	2	3	4			5	6	7	8
9					10				
11				12					
13							14		
			15				16		
17	18	19				20			
21				22					
23				24			25	26	27
28			29						
30						31			
32						33			

ANSWERS ON PAGE 181

IT'S A HIT!

ACROSS

1. Bananas, so to speak
4. Ibsen's Gabler
9. Dentists' org.
10. Bubbling in the pot
11. Festive centerpiece
13. Creator of Genesis
14. Yoga class accessory
15. Slow-moving reptile
18. Find a gusher
21. Cuts back, as bushes
22. Prefix meaning "wine"
23. Cave ricochet
27. Invoke good luck: Colloq.
30. Pianist's practice piece
31. Formerly, in wedding news
32. Hulu offering
33. Masthead figures, for short

DOWN

1. Street guides
2. Together, in music
3. "Drat!" alternative
4. "Like that'll ever happen!"
5. Go back, like the tide
6. Destine for, as failure
7. Hindu festival of lights
8. Wireless company bought by Verizon
12. "The ___ the Hat" (Seuss book)
16. Hawaiian guitar, for short
17. Do over, as a hem
18. Like questions for Siri
19. Number of days in Avril
20. Become depleted
24. Ice cream container
25. Broke up soil

26. Works of Shelley

28. Chi. summer hours

29. "The Wonder Years" teen, for short

1	2	3		4	5	6	7	8
9				10				
11			12					
13						14		
			15	16	17			
18	19	20						
21								
22					23	24	25	26
27			28	29				
30						31		
32						33		

ANSWERS ON PAGE 181

SIGNS, SIGNS, SIGNS

ACROSS

1. "A horse walks into ___ ..."
5. Qatar's qapital
9. Vatican VIP
10. Cabinet dept. with an atom on its seal
11. Remarkable events holding a sign?
13. Dr. Seuss character who "speaks for the trees"
14. Dernier ___ (latest thing)
15. Eels that live in warm seas
17. "What chutzpah!" comment holding an augury?
20. Makes aware
21. Embroidered word on a robe
22. Mixed up
26. "Herstory" topic holding a foreboding word?
28. "The Clan of the Cave Bear" author
29. Comic Fey
30. Letter opening
31. Sign of things to come in 11-, 17-, and 26-Across

DOWN

1. GE stove or fridge
2. ___-chic (hippie-influenced style)
3. Imitative one
4. Changes a moniker
5. FDR or JFK, politically
6. Like a small garage
7. Source of "Once more unto the breach"
8. Ask for ___: request more pay
12. Rhodes scholar, e.g.
16. Has as a tenant
17. "Uh" sounds
18. "Certainly, Monsieur!"
19. Hypnotism pioneer Franz
23. Highly unlikely, as chances
24. One, in Leipzig
25. Impose ___ on (outlaw)
27. Golf champ Ernie

ANSWERS ON PAGE 182

LETTER CHANGE

ACROSS

1. Tall shade trees
5. Marksman's aid
10. Bucks' mates
11. Force forward
12. Lots and lots, or a royal flush
14. One of the Stooges
15. Like an aristocrat
16. Bowler's targets
17. Sushi condiment
20. Poetic tribute
23. Comment after a fine repast
25. Adjust the margins again
26. Haze or gloom
27. "Strawberry Wine" country singer Carter
28. Baby salamanders

DOWN

1. Cheese in a red coat
2. CBS eye, e.g.
3. "A ___ pittance!"
4. Chicago-to-Miami dir.
5. "Happy Days" catchphrase
6. USN bigwigs
7. Newspaper opinion piece
8. Bell's ring
9. "Beverly Hillbillies" daughter ___ May
13. "Open sesame" speaker
16. Song of joyful praise
17. Political district
18. "A Death In The Family" author
19. Spanish girl: abbr.

20. Egg, on a French menu

21. Missile in a pub game

22. Members of BPOE

24. Mrs., in Marseilles

1	2	3	4	■	5	6	7	8	9
10				■	11				
12				13					
14			■	15					
■	■	■	16				■	■	■
17	18	19				■	20	21	22
23						24			
25					■	26			
27					■	28			

ANSWERS ON PAGE 182

SWITCH IT UP

ACROSS

1. Feet in a pound?
5. Paper bags
10. Dentist in "Little Shop of Horrors"
11. ___ Thompson, aka Honey Boo Boo
12. City famed for its tower
13. Luth. or Meth., e.g.
14. Certain untouchables
16. Class for U.S. newcomers
17. Bambi's aunt
18. "Registered" corp. symbols
21. Beverage with scones
23. Altar promises
28. Concur
29. Word before code or rug
30. Kingly sphere
31. Check the bar code
32. Utah state flowers
33. Sailors or old salts

DOWN

1. Bubble wrap sounds
2. Diva's song
3. Madison's state, briefly
4. Catch by trickery
5. Got a horse ready for riding
6. Guinness who played Obi-Wan
7. "Pocahontas" watercraft
8. Like an open secret
9. Kafka character Gregor
15. Thinks highly of
18. Russian rulers of yore
19. "Dirty Dingus ___" (1970 film)
20. Gaunt fellow
22. "Stop!" in piratespeak
24. Change cities, in realtor-speak
25. Willy or Shamu
26. Have on, as clothes
27. ___ souci (carefree)

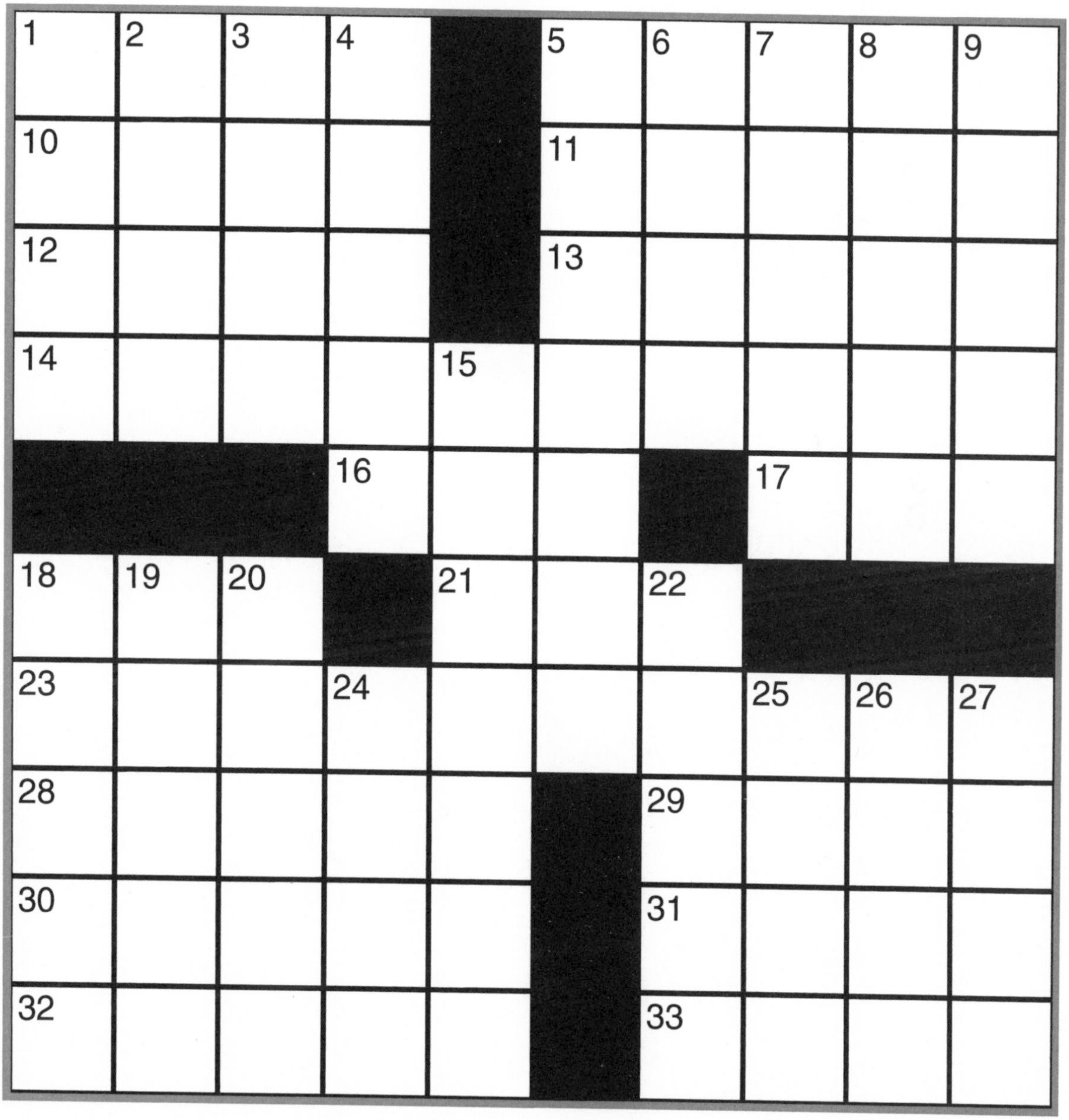

ANSWERS ON PAGE 182

ALTERED SEQUENCE

ACROSS

1. Retirement place?
4. Military decorations
10. Kayaker's need
11. Lisbon's peninsula
12. Popular Thanksgiving veggies
14. Indirectly insulting
15. Wanna-___ (copycats)
16. Language that gave us "khaki"
19. Parent of The Huffington Post
22. Political debate topic
26. Musical neighbor on Captain Kangaroo, with "Mr."
29. "The Breakfast Club" actor Estevez
30. "Be gone!"
31. Mariners
32. Alf and Mork, for short

DOWN

1. Cranberry fields
2. Acquire the old-fashioned way
3. Berlin trio
4. Clementine's father, by occupation
5. Fall away, as a tide
6. Mark to improve
7. Disney's Aladdin or Jafar
8. Rehearsal request
9. Be cheeky with
13. Academic e-mail suffix
17. French mustard
18. Not waste

19. Grows older
20. "It's either him ___"
    (beau's ultimatum)
21. "Star Wars" character
    who kills Jabba
23. Minty herb
24. Foot, fathom, or furlong
25. Approx. figures
27. Movie street
28. Never, in Nuremberg

1	2	3		4	5	6	7	8	9
10				11					
12			13						
14							15		
			16		17	18			
19	20	21			22		23	24	25
26			27	28					
29							30		
31							32		

ANSWERS ON PAGE 182

GO TOGETHER

ACROSS

1. Razor targets
6. Georgia specialty
11. In regard to
12. The king, in France
13. Hard candies
15. Leaning to the right?
16. Spots on TV
17. Geological period
20. Newspaper staffers, for short
23. Classic German 35mm cameras
27. Crooks and felons
30. Deliver a formal speech
31. Do an usher's job
32. Cereal box amt.
33. Curvy letters

DOWN

1. Mecca pilgrim
2. "Like ___ out of ..."
3. "Bridges of Madison County" state
4. Moscow coin
5. Bacon piece
6. The late Mao's group: abbr.
7. Cartoonish squeal
8. Sort of rug or code
9. Bungee jumping need
10. Copperhead sound
14. French school
18. Desist partner
19. Nature walks, e.g.
20. Musk of Tesla
21. Truth or ___ (party game)
22. Police crisis team

24. Gentleman's grades
25. Grammy winner India
26. Common IDs
28. "Incidentally," in a text
29. Abbr. after many an old general's name

1	2	3	4	5		6	7	8	9	10
11						12				
13					14					
15								16		
			17			18	19			
20	21	22			23			24	25	26
27			28	29						
30						31				
32						33				

ANSWERS ON PAGE 183

ANOTHER LETTER CHANGE

ACROSS

1. Book of maps
6. Most Saudis, e.g.
11. Attack on a fort, maybe
12. Berry of "Monster's Ball"
13. Vehement quarrel
15. Bygone Spanish coin
16. Ave. crossers, often
17. Present day figure?
20. English majors' degs.
23. Decorative
27. Process of taking turns
30. Campbell or Watts
31. French door
32. Bus terminal
33. Contemptuous look

DOWN

1. "Right away" letters
2. Kitchen flooring piece
3. Tennis do-overs
4. Author James and baseballer Tommie
5. Big name in mattresses
6. "Eureka!"
7. Deserter of a sinking ship
8. Father-daughter boxers
9. Blemish
10. Capitol VIPs
14. Minolta rival
18. Golf course hazards
19. Chekhov of letters
20. It may be brass or rubber
21. Winglike things
22. Command at a corner
24. Million or billion suffix

25. Carry by hand
26. Cabinet dept. formed under Carter

28. Angsty rock genre
29. Big name in home dyes

1	2	3	4	5		6	7	8	9	10
11						12				
13				14						
15								16		
		17			18	19				
20	21	22		23			24	25	26	
27			28	29						
30						31				
32						33				

ANSWERS ON PAGE 183

MAKING WAVES

ACROSS

1. Flat-bottomed rowboat
6. Kind of steamer
11. Prefix for net or national
12. Actress Skye and others
13. Common sight in Alaskan waters
15. Device for the deaf, for short
16. Nymphs of Greek myth
17. Country music's LeAnn
19. Cruise locales
22. Little green men, for short
25. Regatta entrant
28. Win by ___ (barely defeat)
29. First name in cosmetics
30. Cruise ship
31. One-masted sailboat

DOWN

1. Put through a sieve
2. Heal, as bones
3. "The ___-bitsy spider…"
4. Exclamation akin to "yuck"
5. "Casual" dress day: abbr.
6. Big cat, in Barcelona
7. Judicial gowns
8. Buffalo of the Celebes
9. "Coming of Age in Samoa" author
10. Sounds for attention
14. Chinese menu notation
17. Paycheck upgrade
18. Kind of sanctum or circle
19. Like folk traditions
20. "What more ___ say?"
21. Subj. for Milton Friedman

22. Prefix for -plasm or -derm   26. Positive reply

23. Kojak, to friends   27. Manual alphabet, briefly

24. Dance move

1	2	3	4	5	■	6	7	8	9	10
11					■	12				
13					14					
15			■	■	16					
■	■	■	17	18				■	■	■
19	20	21				■	■	22	23	24
25						26	27			
28					■	29				
30					■	31				

ANSWERS ON PAGE 183

NAME THE PLAY

ACROSS

1. Criminal's fake name
6. Early auto starter
11. Height's companion
12. Everglades wader
13. Shakespeare play with Touchstone
15. Healthy salad choice
16. Mountain nymphs
17. Class for new U.S. immigrants
18. Not straight
19. Colony critters
20. Hindu term of respect
23. Two-time Best Actress Jackson
26. Front of the leg
27. Shakespeare play with Leontes and Perdita, with "The"
29. Home of the Ewoks
30. Less bananas?
31. Midday times
32. Grab forcefully

DOWN

1. Like an insomniac
2. Simpson and Kudrow
3. Pastoral poem
4. Stick ___ in (test the waters)
5. Moo-pork link on a Chinese menu
6. Cricket sounds
7. Enter again, as text
8. Kind of code or rug
9. Reason for denying entry, maybe
10. Some chessmen: abbr.
14. Cigarette ad claim
18. Thermometer developer Celsius
19. Author Chekhov
20. Classic Ladd western
21. Annoys, with "up"
22. Chemically inactive
23. "The Voice" judge Stefani
24. Kitchen floor, to a Brit
25. Inner: prefix

26. Sky light

28. Opp. of NNE

1	2	3	4	5	■	6	7	8	9	10
11					■	12				
13					14					
15				■	16					
17			■	18				■	■	■
■	■	■	19				■	20	21	22
23	24	25				■	26			
27						28				
29					■	30				
31					■	32				

MATH JOKES

ACROSS

1. Have ___ face (be embarrassed)
5. Carpenter's groove
9. End of a pasta brand name
10. "Let's go!"
11. Old mathematicians never die, they just lose some of their...
13. "Must-___" (old NBC slogan)
14. Afternoon snooze
15. Lorre's "Casablanca" character
17. Algebra jokes are so...
20. Dissertation
21. Congressman, for short
22. Gave out meds
26. Hear about the statistician who drowned crossing a river? It was 3 feet deep...
28. "... ___ it Memorex?"
29. Desert dweller
30. Arsonist, slangily
31. Talese and Goldin

DOWN

1. Sandy's lines, in "Annie"
2. Rakish sort
3. Feminizing suffix
4. Formal orders
5. 601, in old Rome
6. Egyptian Sun God
7. Italian astronomer who discovered six comets
8. How freelancers may work
12. Couch potato's must-have mag
16. Losing candidate
17. Old sitcom set at Fort Courage
18. "The Gift of the Magi" author
19. Mr. Fixit's forte
23. "Love Song" singer Bareilles

24. Eddie who inspired "The French Connection"

25. Coming-out gals

27. Letters on a brandy label

1	2	3	4	■	5	6	7	8
9				■	10			
11				12				
13					■	14		
■	■	■	15		16			
17	18	19						
20						■	■	■
21			■	22		23	24	25
26			27					
28				■	29			
30				■	31			

ANSWERS ON PAGE 184

OLÉ!

ACROSS

1. Simpson imp
5. $\frac{1}{16}$ of a cup, briefly
9. Slangy "okay"
10. Cashmere or angora
11. Tribal carving in the Northwest
13. As a friend, in Paris
14. Maude player Arthur
15. Stella ___ (beer)
17. Hamlet, Gandhi, or Forrest Gump
20. Marcos with a lot of shoes
21. Student's stat
22. Early Peruvians
26. Flatfish often served pan-seared
28. Keats's poems
29. Kind of exam or history
30. Beatty and Kelly
31. Cry like a kitten

DOWN

1. Eight bits to computer folk
2. "___ Flux" (Charlize Theron film)
3. "Pro" follower
4. Teen hangout
5. County div., at times
6. Child's owie
7. "Cirque du ___"
8. "The magic word," to tots
12. Caught up by, as debt
16. Window above a door
17. Offspring of a male tiger and female lion
18. Slow the progress of
19. Combined forces
23. Central part
24. What there "oughta be"
25. Trading floor call
27. CIA forerunner

ANSWERS ON PAGE 184

RHYME TIME

ACROSS

1. Ceiling timber
5. Old Glory bar
11. Like some "shoppes"
12. Mountain bush
13. Form-fitting casual wear
15. Barcelona's country, to natives
16. Bus depot, for short
17. Elon Musk company
20. 1988 buyer of Motown
23. Big arteries
27. In high spirits
30. White mouse, e.g.
31. Arabian Sea gulf
32. Elon Musk company
33. Rip and crosscut

DOWN

1. Big name in home audio
2. "Benevolent" fraternal order
3. Go for ___ (swim)
4. ___ Work (road sign)
5. Quite cunning, in a simile
6. Mahal of fame
7. Regret deeply
8. Kin of 401(k)s
9. Bottled (up)
10. Anna's sister in "Frozen"
14. It's opposite SSW
18. Arced, soft throw
19. Neighborhoods
20. Painters' degs.
21. Robert of "I Spy"
22. "Fantastic Four" actress Jessica

24. "And there it is!"
25. From the start again
26. 9-digit IDs

28. Driver's ID
29. Yearling's age

1	2	3	4		5	6	7	8	9	10
11					12					
13				14						
15								16		
			17			18	19			
20	21	22			23			24	25	26
27			28	29						
30							31			
32							33			

ANSWERS ON PAGE 184

RIDDLES

ACROSS

1. Bausch & ___ (eye-care brand)
5. LAPD alerts
9. Bitsy preceder
10. The thing there
11. What kind of horse only comes out on Halloween? A...
13. In ___ (fretful)
14. Between Sault and Marie
15. Greek sea
17. What did the skeleton buy at the market?
20. "It's everywhere you ___ be" (Visa slogan)
21. Feet above sea level: abbr.
22. Cuddly creatures in "Return of the Jedi"
26. Where does Dracula keep his money? In the...
28. Bugaboo
29. "Greetings, sailor!"
30. River of Flanders
31. Gumption

DOWN

1. Director Wertmuller ("Seven Beauties")
2. Cole Porter's "Miss ___ Regrets"
3. High-ranking NCO
4. From memory
5. Dough dispenser, briefly
6. Beginning stage of a study
7. Drinker's bill
8. Some Dutch masterpieces
12. Sent a message to one's "followers"
16. Gardener's fabric planter for cucumbers, sweet peppers, etc.
17. Sailor
18. Bust on which Poe's raven perched
19. San ___ (Spurs' home, slangliy)
23. Diamond Head island

24. Lumber flaw
25. "The ___ the limit!"

27. Poets' above

1	2	3	4		5	6	7	8
9					10			
11				12				
13						14		
			15		16			
17	18	19						
20								
21				22		23	24	25
26			27					
28					29			
30					31			

ANSWERS ON PAGE 184

SEUSS FOR YOUSE

ACROSS

1. Concluding passage, in music
5. Administered, as medicine
10. Having no width or depth
11. To be, in Acapulco
12. "Fiddling" emperor
13. Bring cheer to
14. Seuss character who's a toothless jellyfish in "The Tooth Book"
16. "It's the end of an ___"
17. Hospital VIPS
18. Mama bear, in Madrid
21. "Atlas Shrugged" novelist Rand
23. Seuss book about a character who speaks in tongue twisters
28. Highland dance
29. Run into
30. Duck, as an issue
31. Chick follower?
32. Moves, in real estate jargon
33. Bumper ding

DOWN

1. And, if, or but: abbr.
2. "Dedicated to the ___ Love" (Mamas & the Papas hit)
3. Skin: prefix
4. Brick of clay and straw
5. Spinners at parties
6. Capital of Norway
7. Music holder
8. Chow hound
9. Get togged out
15. Florida fruit
18. Negotiator's proposal
19. Complete, as this puzzle
20. Like the rotation of the earth
22. Wandering one
24. Prefix with "China"

25. Formally hand over
26. Sharp, as vision

27. Leave in, as text

1	2	3	4		5	6	7	8	9
10					11				
12					13				
14				15					
			16				17		
18	19	20		21		22			
23			24				25	26	27
28						29			
30						31			
32						33			

ANSWERS ON PAGE 185

SMALL CHANGE

ACROSS

1. Bar code swipes
6. Luxury auto, for short
11. Eagle's lair
12. Savory scent
13. Tidy sum, slangily
15. Center of a square, often
16. Dawn goddess
17. Bridge player's "no bid"
20. "Orphan Annie" protector
23. Brought up
27. Brake quickly
30. Barbershop voice
31. Implied but unspoken
32. Altar settings
33. Top bananas

DOWN

1. Drains, as strength
2. Tic-Tac alternative
3. Region
4. Capone henchman Frank
5. Frame, in a bad way
6. Hip-hop sound
7. Gold or silver source
8. Kind of wolf
9. KP sandwich?
10. Declares
14. Hanker (for)
18. Does an usher's job
19. Egyptian president Anwar
20. "The Thin Man" dog
21. Dance move
22. Late soprano Lily
24. Costa ___ (Nicaragua neighbor)

25. Muslim prince

26. Sleuths: abbr.

28. "Annabel Lee" poet

29. Surg. facilities

1	2	3	4	5		6	7	8	9	10
11						12				
13				14						
15								16		
			17			18	19			
20	21	22			23			24	25	26
27			28	29						
30						31				
32						33				

ANSWERS ON PAGE 185

TEMPERATURE RISING

ACROSS

1. Inform on, slangily
7. Gulager of "The Virginian"
10. Newspaper publisher Ochs
11. Not at all nerdy
12. Headgear commonly worn by rice farmers
14. It is, in Spain
15. Dressing choice
16. Crow's-nest cry
17. Exercise outfit
21. Inane behavior
22. Fred's best friend on "Sanford and Son"
23. Mother Earth
27. Common meeting place
29. Carrere of 'Wayne's orld'
30. "My sentiments exactly"
31. Wall and 42nd: abbr.
32. German submarines

DOWN

1. Track event
2. Bustling times
3. Hit the horn
4. ___ podrida (Spanish stew)
5. AP rival, once
6. Psychologist's treatment
7. Old radio's "___the Magician"
8. Brittle-shelled Chinese nut
9. End result
13. Brinker with storied skates
16. "Charlie's Angels" actress
17. Ghostly creatures, in poetry
18. Good with one's hands
19. Rodeo ropes
20. A la ___ (with ice cream)
23. Type of dancer in a disco
24. Magic-spell starter
25. Skeptical response
26. Sailors' affirmatives
28. Research facility, for short

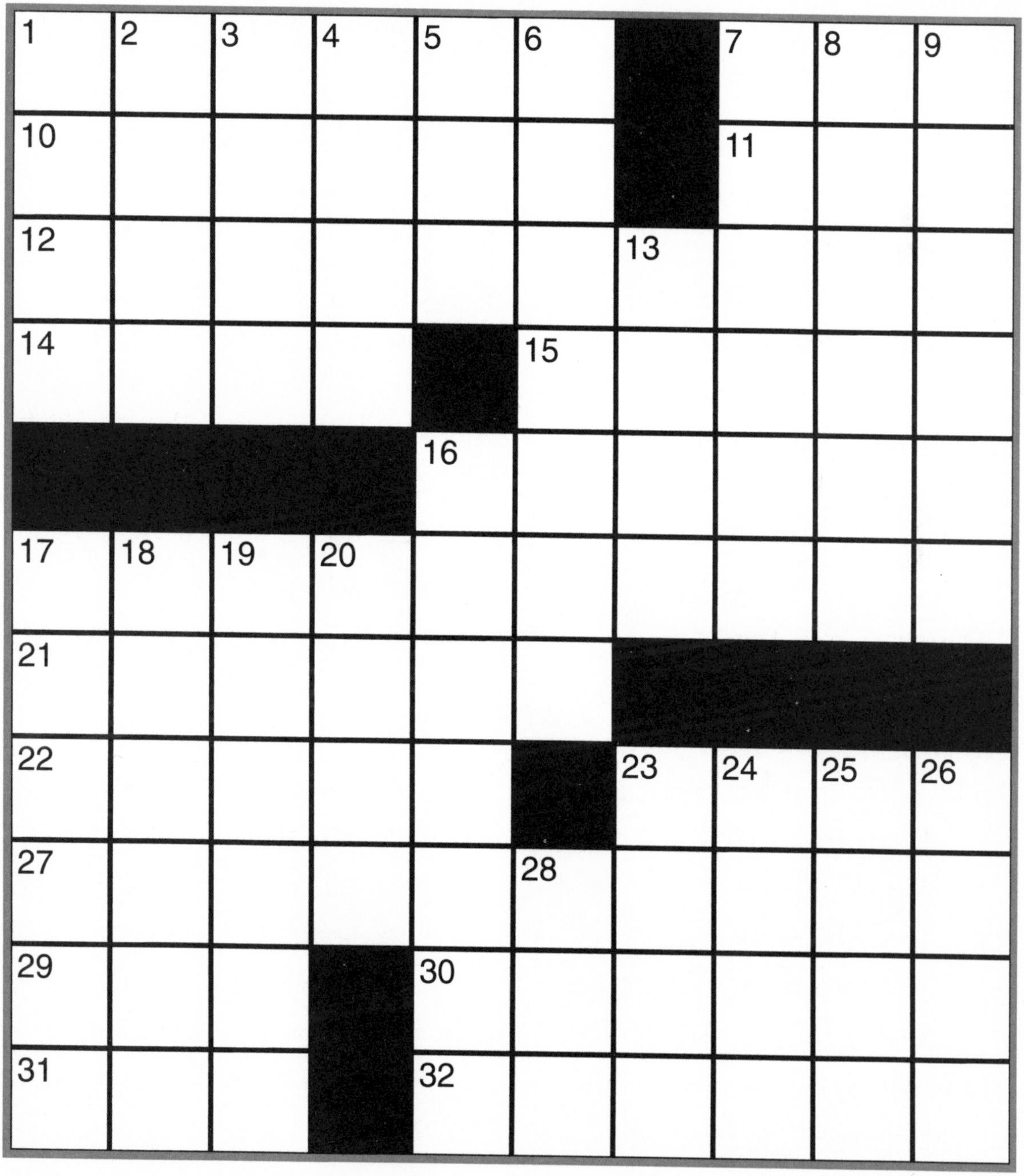

ANSWERS ON PAGE 185

QUICK COUNT

ACROSS

1. Closes with a bang
6. Inebriate
11. What a Parisian smokes
12. Outside: Prefix
13. "Again!"
15. Handheld computer before tablets
16. Barracks bed
17. Mo. for hobgoblins
18. Sooner St.
19. "Bravo!"
23. Hasty, as a decision
24. No, to a Scot
25. DSL provider
26. "In all probability..."
30. 1986 film starring Martin Short, Steve Martin, and Chevy Chase
32. Change, as text
33. Cases for pins, needles, etc.
34. California's Point ___ National Seashore
35. Spiral-horned antelope

DOWN

1. Word in a red octagon
2. Clark's Smallville girlfriend
3. First shepherd
4. Elephant ancestor
5. Word with tape or whiskey
6. Pager signal
7. Abbr. after a telephone number
8. Adheres
9. Brass that resembles gold
10. Keep the beat with your feet
14. Capitol feature
18. Big problem?
19. More hackneyed
20. Message on a dusty car
21. Fish-catching raptor
22. AMC drama with Jon Hamm
26. Brit. reference works

27. Mexican water
28. Churn and bubble
29. Early weather satellite
31. Compass dir. near
    2 o'clock

1	2	3	4	5	■	6	7	8	9	10
11					■	12				
13				14						
15						■	16			
■	■	17			■	18				
19	20	21			22					
23				■	24			■	■	■
25			■	26				27	28	29
30		31								
32					■	33				
34					■	35				

ANSWERS ON PAGE 185

RHYME IT

ACROSS

1. Heaps
6. Beauty queen's topper
11. Words after "like it" and "ready"
12. Rombauer and La Douce
13. Bag IDs
15. Peas' place
16. 66, famously: Abbr.
17. Kin of calc. and geom.
18. Mosquito cousin
19. Tibetan streamers
23. Do-overs, in tennis
24. Major time period
25. GI's hangout
26. Kimono-clad hostesses
30. Recurring jokes used for cumulative comic effect
32. "He doesn't have ___ bone in his body"
33. Restaurants with orange roofs, familiarly
34. Brought about
35. Makeup of some nests

DOWN

1. Scale notes after fas
2. Motley ___ (Nikki Sixx's band)
3. Cherub at Notre Dame
4. Sultry part of summer
5. Basic commodity
6. Headed for overtime
7. First NYC subway
8. Cuneiform discovery site
9. Like a hodgepodge
10. Cash, stocks and charm, e.g.
14. Install solar panels, say
18. Scotland's largest city
19. "Cacti" or "stimuli," e.g.
20. Go back to a task
21. Made amends (for)
22. Sudden scare
26. Marchetti of football fame
27. Mecca pilgrim
28. Crazy over
29. Worrisome sound for a balloonist

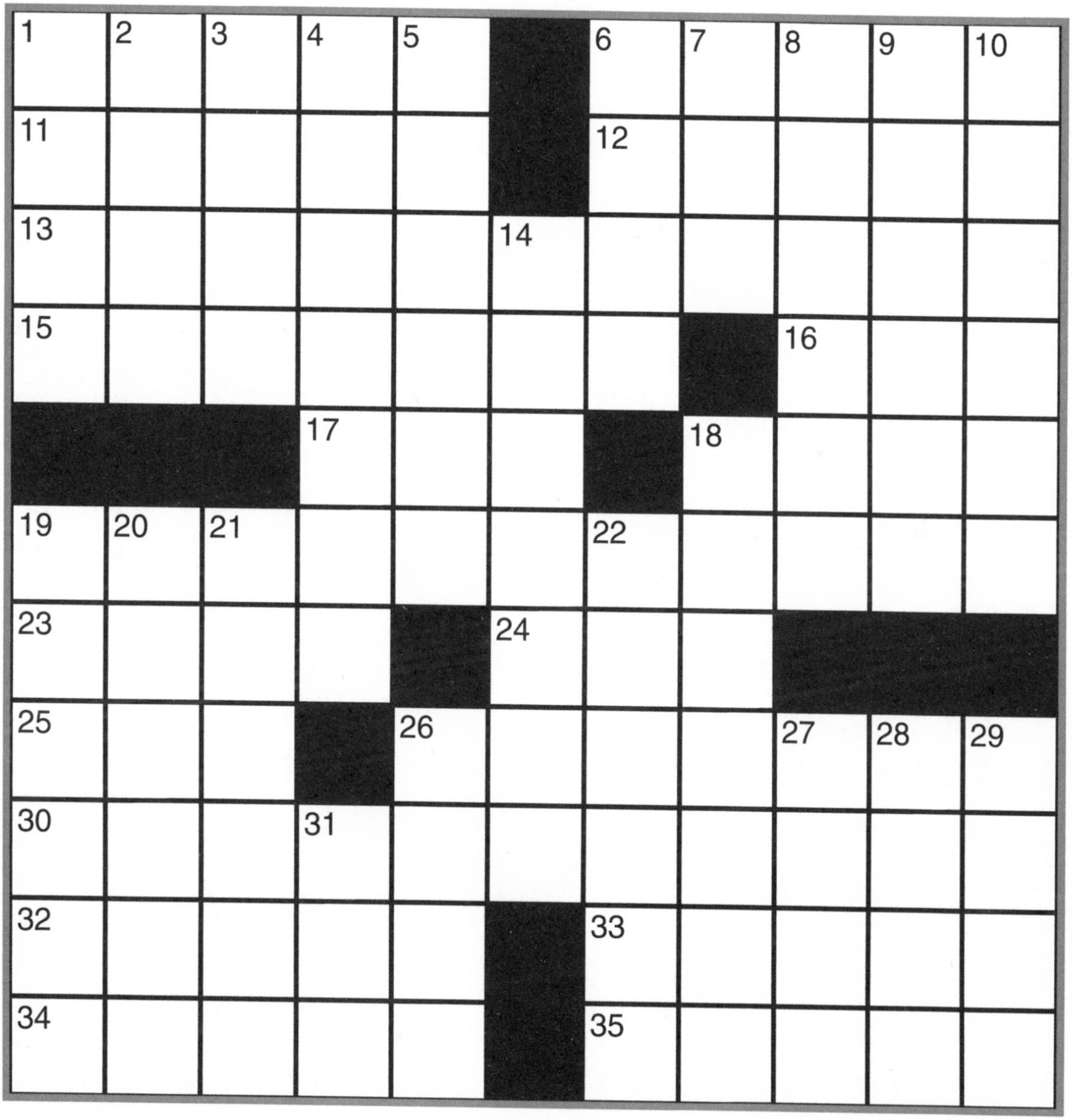

TERMS OF ART

ACROSS

1. Like unwelcome criticism
6. Cass and Michelle, in '60s pop
11. Hello or goodbye, in one state
12. Eye-bending paintings
13. Term for paintings of elegantly dressed groups at play in rural settings
15. Cressida's love
16. Prot., for example
17. Do-over, in tennis
18. Ostracize
19. Term for contrast of light and shade in art
23. Suffixes with "ball" and "bass"
24. Lowdown sort
25. Old sofa problem
26. Trouser that resembles a skirt
30. Term for art so realistic it can "fool the eye"
32. Ad ___ per aspera (Kansas motto)
33. Word of mock horror
34. Takes a break
35. Hercules slew its lion

DOWN

1. Axe handle
2. Angel or Royal, briefly
3. Old paper section
4. Aussie lassies
5. Boxing's "Marvelous Marvin"
6. Atomic groups: Abbr.
7. Therapists' org.
8. Fu ___ (kind of mustache)
9. Camelot king
10. Camp cook's fuel
14. Teleprompter
18. Dickens miser
19. One sharing top billing
20. Husky, as a voice
21. Gold bars
22. In a gloomy mood
26. Tax experts, for short

27. Mets, Nets or Jets

28. It comes in waves

29. "Frozen" character

31. "I pity the fool!" speaker

1	2	3	4	5		6	7	8	9	10
11						12				
13					14					
15								16		
			17				18			
19	20	21				22				
23					24					
25				26				27	28	29
30			31							
32						33				
34						35				

ANSWERS ON PAGE 186

THINGS WE GOT FROM THE BRITS

ACROSS

1. Bedside ringer
6. He held the whole world in his hands
11. Inverted "v"
12. German wine valley
13. British mathematician Charles Babbage's "analytical engine" gave us this
15. Disappearing lake of Asia
16. Nashville awards org.
17. Springsteen's birthplace, in song
18. Model in a bottle
19. Snack named for an English earl
23. Give an edge to
24. Boy's name in a Johnny Cash title
25. Relative of yore
26. Broadcast schedule item
30. English inventor Alexander Cumming got the first patent for this
32. Body part often sculpted
33. Cool red giant
34. Clean with a broom
35. Soda fountain order

DOWN

1. ___ part (play on stage)
2. Cowardly Lion player
3. Neck of the woods
4. Hermit
5. Greek peak
6. Harp in Roma
7. Day before a "TGIF!" cry
8. Chinese nut
9. In need of iron
10. Angel with six wings
14. Isn't kidding
18. Word with "meatballs" or "massage"
19. Reasons for burglary reports
20. Like some Easter bunnies
21. Have staying power
22. Large red hogs
26. Just ___, skip and a jump
27. High, in place names

28. Deck wood

29. Raison d'___
(reason for being)

31. Chicago-to-Miami dir.

1	2	3	4	5	■	6	7	8	9	10
11					■	12				
13				14						
15						■	16			
■	■	■	17			■	18			
19	20	21				22				
23				■	24			■	■	■
25			■	26				27	28	29
30			31							
32					■	33				
34					■	35				

121

THREE BY KING

ACROSS

1. It should make you pause
6. Ears pricked up
11. "Let me repeat…"
12. More fraught with danger
13. The title of this 1979 Stephen King novel refers to an area of the brain
15. Enters carefully
16. Atom with an electric charge
17. Georgia's capital, casually
18. Litmus reddener
19. 1983 Stephen King horror novel with a misspelled title word
23. "Oysters ___ in season"
24. Architect's wing
25. Bygone French coin
26. Necessarily involves
30. 1980 Stephen King novel about a young girl who develops pyrokinesis
32. Concerning, old-style
33. "___ Kick Out of You" (Cole Porter song)
34. Minstrel poets
35. Monopoly payments

DOWN

1. Issue a ticket to
2. Agcy. concerned with work hazards
3. Fannie ___ (securities)
4. Israel's region
5. "___ Fideles": carol
6. Arith. chore
7. Actress Taylor, familiarly
8. Beethoven's 3rd Symphony
9. "Girl With a Hoop" painter
10. Hot, for now
14. Cold, for one
18. Like escaped convicts
19. Modular, as a home
20. Live oak of California
21. One seeing the sights
22. 1975 microcomputer, the ___ 8800

26. Ballpark figures: Abbr.

27. Calif.-to-Fla. highway

28. Native of Latvia

29. Ladies of Spain, briefly

31. What this is for the down clues

1	2	3	4	5		6	7	8	9	10
11						12				
13					14					
15								16		
			17				18			
19	20	21				22				
23					24					
25				26				27	28	29
30			31							
32						33				
34						35				

ANSWERS ON PAGE 186

SIX AUTHORS

ACROSS

1. "A Death in the Family" author
5. "Watership Down" author
10. Kind of atty.
11. Hawaii's "Garden Island"
12. "The Catcher in the Rye" author
14. Quiet ending?
15. Where Ottawa is: abbr.
16. Zipped past, or offered for feedback
18. Brain scans, for short
22. Cousin of a foil
23. Uninhabited land, often
24. Agcy. that aids mom-and-pop stores
26. "That's ___-brainer!"
27. "The Lord of the Rings" author
31. "Hunter" in the sky
32. About, in a memo
33. "The Da Vinci Code" author
34. "Coming of Age in Samoa" author

DOWN

1. Command earnestly
2. Command to a horse
3. Ancient Semite
4. JFK estimate
5. Closely related (to)
6. "The Count of Monte Cristo" hero
7. Eighth cal. page
8. Dogpatch's Daisy ___
9. "To ___, With Love," Poitier film
13. "The Thin Man" co-star Myrna
17. Present, as a gift
19. "Seinfeld" gal pal
20. They're divided into species
21. What Goliath got
23. Suffix with resident or president
25. Former capital of West Germany

27. Biblical symbol of patience
28. Growling sound
29. Olympics host of 2016, for short
30. Kipling novel about an orphan boy

1	2	3	4		5	6	7	8	9
10					11				
12				13					
14				15					
16			17			18	19	20	21
22					23				
			24	25			26		
27	28	29				30			
31						32			
33						34			

ANSWERS ON PAGE 187

SUMMER FUN

ACROSS

1. Hearts or darts
5. Beach find
10. Hot spot in the kitchen
11. Bear on a bed
12. Beach construction
14. Grand Central, e.g.: abbr.
15. Buddy, slangily
16. "Othello" villain and "Aladdin" parrot
18. West Point, for short
22. White House VIP
23. Playful swimmer
24. Little one
26. Former Mideast org.
27. Nice place to walk along
31. Be ___ (constantly complain)
32. Goes flat, as a car battery
33. Seascape sights
34. Put in order

DOWN

1. Scuttlebutt
2. Online persona
3. Social unit; household
4. Finish line
5. Tree topper
6. Announcer's call after three strikes
7. Mass. summer hrs.
8. "Bad" cholesterol, for short
9. Harsh cleanser
13. "Survivor" network
17. Bone-related
19. Artist's workplace
20. Far from plentiful
21. Cop's collar
23. They may follow the 4th qtr.
25. Crystal balls, e.g.
27. "Fuzzy Wuzzy ___ a bear"
28. Here, in Madrid
29. Bi- plus one
30. Singers Ames and Sheeran

ANSWERS ON PAGE 187

ACROSS

1. Epic tale
5. Splashy party on many a cruise
9. Dishonest types
11. "Sounds like fun!"
12. On ___ (counting calories)
13. "Atlas Shrugged" author
14. Splashy activity on many a cruise ship
16. Back muscle, to a gym rat
17. "___ Boot" (1981 war film)
18. A time to remember
21. "Apocalypse Now" setting, briefly
23. Entertainment on most cruise ships
28. Follow commands
29. Be crazy about
30. Cunard ___ (QE2's cruise operator)
31. ___ powder (flee)
32. Some pass receivers
33. What parallel lines don't do

DOWN

1. KFC side order
2. Slave girl of opera
3. Pace or trot
4. Whirling, old-style
5. Tomorrow's woman
6. "The way of a man with ___" (Bible)
7. Hunt of "NCIS: Los Angeles"
8. South America's "spine"
10. London theater street
15. Patronize, as an inn
18. School, in France
19. Hood of renown
20. Make a change to
22. CBS's "___ Secretary"
24. Peer group?
25. Pepsi rival
26. Word with family or fruit
27. Straphanger's lack

COMFORT FOOD

ACROSS

1. Word with "fry" or "potatoes"
6. Main Street liners
10. Capital of Vietnam
11. Bell sound
12. Friend, in Mexico
13. Sicilian top-blower
14. Popular breakfast order
16. Drill sgt. e.g.
17. "How beautiful!"
18. Psychological org.
21. "Gross!"
23. Popular 14-Across go-with
28. "Born Free" lioness
29. "For want of ___, the shoe was lost"
30. Track and field event
31. Kramer of "Seinfeld"
32. Tipplers
33. Backspace through text

DOWN

1. Former leader of Iran
2. Call from the crib
3. Like cartoon movies: abbr.
4. Boston's airport
5. Simba, at the beginning of the film
6. Fencing blade
7. Release one's grip
8. Chutney fruit
9. Diagonal line
15. Greyhound competition
18. Polite coughs
19. Caveman-style, as a diet
20. Item in black ink
22. Present with a medal, say
24. Things going to your head?
25. "That ___ close one!"
26. "___ Island" (Jodie Foster film)
27. Blackthorn plum, gin flavoring

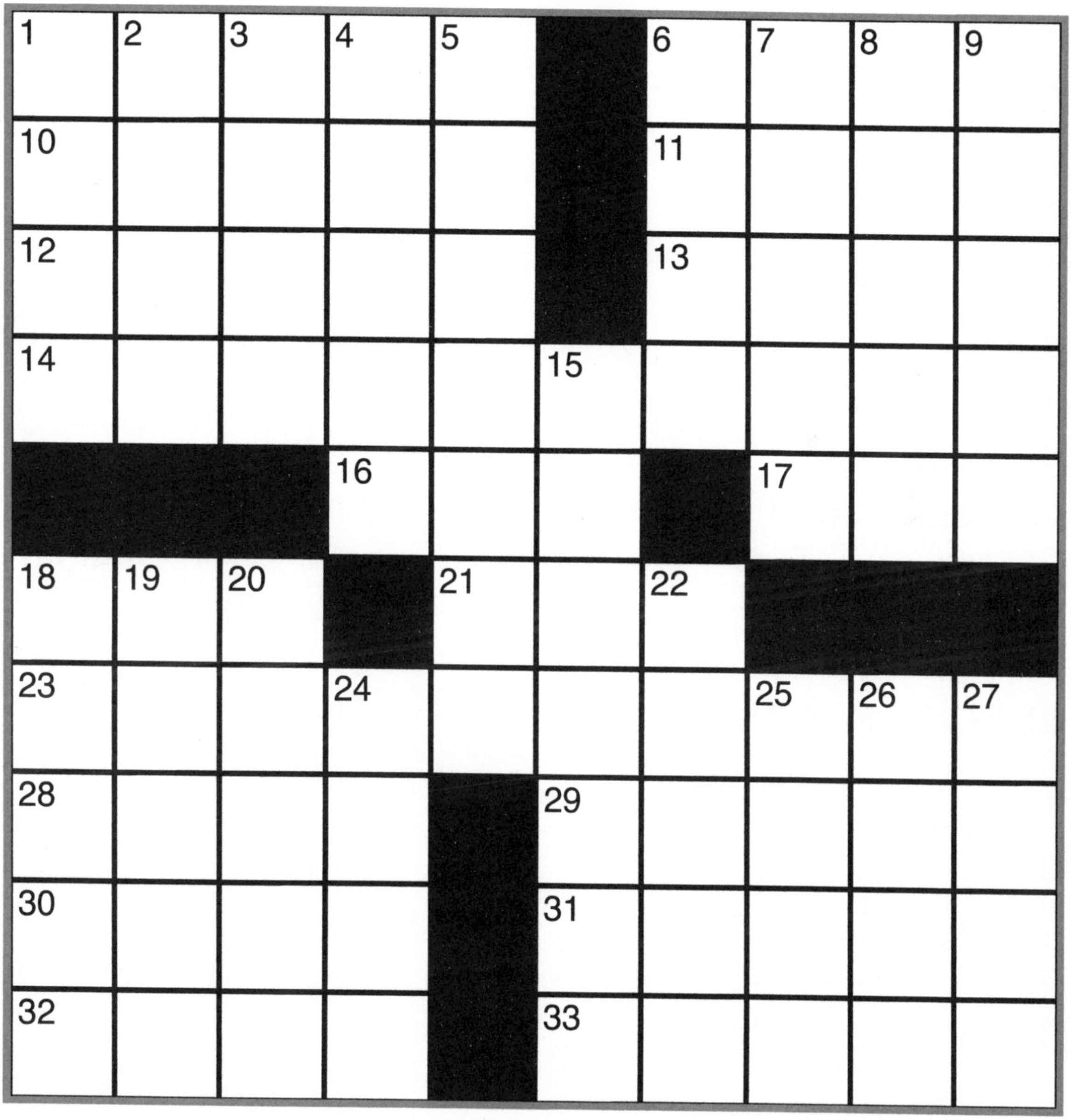

ANSWERS ON PAGE 187

BOUNCING BACK

ACROSS

1. Parisian eatery
7. Closely related
11. Pop open, as champagne
12. Like a house pet
13. "No Exit" author
14. "I Am Not My Hair" singer India.___
15. Genuflecting joint
16. Boy's chore
18. Catch sight of
19. Score perfectly on a test
20. Chatty ___ (early talking doll)
22. Clairvoyance letters
25. Hawaiian thanks
27. Sound hiding in 3-, 6-, and 8-Down
28. Michelle of "Crouching Tiger, Hidden Dragon"
29. Crocodile tears
31. "... ___ will all hang separately"
32. Get by intimidation
33. Like darker typeface
34. Gets hitched in haste

DOWN

1. Sings on the sidewalk
2. Really silly
3. Hooter, hiding a cave sound?
4. Bag for shopping
5. School basics, briefly
6. Florida's largest lake, hiding a tunnel sound effect?
7. Pong pioneer
8. Martial arts blow, hiding a sound bouncing back?
9. "Sure, let's do it"
10. Food or shelter, e.g.
17. "The Bridge of San Luis ___"
19. Bermuda's locale: abbr.
21. Followed a doctor's order?
23. Land along the coast
24. Blog entries
25. Abbr. that means "Butt out!"

26. Word with dynamic or space

27. Suffix for palm

30. Guns N' Roses rocker ___ Rose

1	2	3	4	5	6	■	7	8	9	10
11						■	12			
13						■	14			
15				■	16	17				
18			■	19					■	
■		20	21				■	22	23	24
25	26					■	27			
28				■	29	30				
31				■	32					
33				■	34					

ANSWERS ON PAGE 188

CITES IN SONG

ACROSS

1. Golden Gate suspender
6. High-tech spy plane acronym
11. Related to a hipbone
12. "Well, lah-___!"
13. City song in "The Music Man"
15. High-tech valley
16. Army guys, for short
17. It's picked by the picky
18. Ice cream purchase
19. City before "Choo Choo" in a Glenn Miller song
23. With -phile, a wine lover
24. Craggy summit
25. Elton John's label, once
26. Stake for a shelter
30. "A Bar in ___": Merle Haggard song
32. "There is ___ in the affairs of men" (Shakespeare)
33. Speedy Amtrak train
34. Has an inclination (to)
35. Slave girl in "Uncle Tom's Cabin"

DOWN

1. Butts, in brief
2. Jai ___ (fast court game)
3. Rotate floating logs
4. Scold harshly
5. Draw forth
6. Building annex: abbr.
7. Rival of PlayStation 3
8. Graceful dance
9. Chair repairer's work
10. California lake, dam, county, and peak
14. Writes the score for
18. Colonnaded entrance
19. Front-line action
20. Goddess of witchcraft
21. Darth Vader's first name
22. Like many diet foods
26. "___ chic!"
27. Comment from a chick
28. Right-angled additions

29. Sydney salutation

31. Longtime TV announcer Hall

1	2	3	4	5		6	7	8	9	10
11						12				
13					14					
15								16		
			17				18			
19	20	21				22				
23					24					
25				26				27	28	29
30			31							
32						33				
34						35				

ANSWERS ON PAGE 188

DOOHICKEYS

ACROSS

1. Utah city named for a Biblical kingdom
5. Precious stone weight
10. He loved an Irish Rose
11. Tropical hat
12. Gizmo
14. Hard to catch
15. Opposite of sml.
16. What two heads are better than
17. Suffix for "arbor" or "ether"
18. Doodad
23. Brain scan, briefly
24. Campers, for short
25. "Volare (___ blu di pinto di blu)"
26. Big-beaked tropical birds
30. Whatchamacallit
32. Epic Virgil poem
33. Go on a tirade
34. Words before golf clubs or silverware
35. Madrid ladies: abbr.

DOWN

1. Chemical spray
2. Ancient Greek coin
3. Aborigine of Japan
4. Plays, as a horse
5. Matador's prop
6. Picnic intruder
7. Complained loudly
8. Ethically challenged
9. Hair snarl
11. It has a hard smooth surface
13. Bilbo Baggins's find
18. Dressed like
19. Tittering sound
20. Like a crystal chandelier
21. Egg cell
22. Film trophies
26. End-of-week initials
27. Slightly open
28. Name hidden in Hirschfeld caricatures
29. Army NCOs
31. Hero of "The Matrix"

ANSWERS ON PAGE 188

ACROSS

1. Emeralds and rubies, e.g.
5. Commando specialties
10. Double-___ (kind of tournament, for short)
11. Issue an order
12. She joined her late father for "Unforgettable"
14. Army amphib vehicle
15. "Hip Hop Is Dead" rapper
16. Tongue-clucking sound
17. "Saturday Night Live" notable Fey
18. Borden mascot
22. Basketball great Archibald
23. Oscar-nominated actor in "The Crying Game"
24. Military leave inits.
25. Van Cleef & ___ (French jewelry house)
29. "No More Mr. Nice Guy" shock-rocker
32. Pontiff's office
33. Backpacker's shelter
34. Cardio-boxing routine
35. "Go ___ Watchman": Harper

DOWN

1. Hollywood's Rowlands
2. Actor Jack of old Westerns
3. Catcher's glove
4. Know-it-all
5. Mr. ___ (old whodunit board game)
6. NCAA division in which Duke plays
7. Darkly humorous
8. FDR's middle name
9. Fun use for a fulcrum
11. Tess Trueheart's love
13. Do some high-tech surgery
17. Kettles kin
18. Captivated
19. The yellow Teletubby
20. Chipmunk feature
21. Damsel's rescuer
26. Fencing sword

27. Hot cross buns season
28. Latina lass, briefly
30. Airport queue vehicle

31. Friendly "green" letters found in 12-, 18-, and 29-Across

1	2	3	4	■	■	5	6	7	8	9
10				■	11					
12				13						
14						■		15		
■	■	■	16			■	17			
18	19	20				21				
22				■	23			■	■	■
24			■		25			26	27	28
29			30	31						
32						■	33			
34					■		35			

ANSWERS ON PAGE 188

ACROSS

1. "Halt!," on the high seas
6. Cracks a book
11. Jazz legend Washington
12. Hercules slew its lion
13. John Grisham's first novel, 1989
15. Star of the recital, often
16. Ending with inter or infer
17. "Quiet, please!"
18. "___-Bungay" (Wells novel)
19. John Grisham 2013 sequel to 13-Across
23. Piggies of verse
24. Bygone New Zealand bird
25. Ending with inter or infer
26. Not well-known
30. John Grisham legal thriller, 2000
32. Ride without pedaling
33. Edit, as text
34. Bagel centers
35. "The defense ___"

DOWN

1. Dickens and Nabokov heroines
2. Actor Danny De___
3. Blue dye plant
4. Indian turnovers
5. Religious belief
6. "Oysters ___ in season"
7. "___ a mouse!"
8. "Fur Elise" key
9. FDR's middle name
10. Pallid
14. Katanga leader Moïse
18. Eager pupil's request
19. Bit of needlework
20. Attention-getting shout
21. Cap'n Crunch, e.g.
22. List of a team's players
26. Dinner scraps
27. Actress Mary and musician Midge
28. Apartment payment
29. Partner of odds
31. Mad cow disease acronym

ANSWERS ON PAGE 189

YOU KNOW MY NAME

ACROSS

1. Site of witch trials
6. Arizona flattops
11. Gaucho's plain
12. Highfalutin'
13. Why should you never mention the number 288?
15. Inlaid-tile designs
16. Stow, with "away"
17. Bank account fig.
18. Expectant fathers do it
19. What did Al Gore play on his guitar?
23. Needlefish
24. About half of all adults
25. Handy thing to know?: abbr.
26. Sticks together
30. Why did the chicken cross the Mobius strip? To get to…
32. Big helicopters, in military slang
33. Choir's specialty
34. "Flip This House" channel
35. Bias, in reporting

DOWN

1. Meager, as chances
2. Certain female voice
3. Aberdeen maiden
4. Involves by necessity
5. Summer yard chore
6. Cosmo and GQ, e.g.
7. Goof up
8. ___ nothing (barge ahead)
9. In and of itself
10. Horse player's strategy
14. Nadya Suleman, in headlines
18. Evergreen-scented cleaner
19. Christie of mysteries
20. New Hampshire city that's also the name of a famous racehorse
21. "America's Funniest People" co-host Sorkin
22. Does more tailoring on, as a skirt

26. Detective's job
27. "Lovely" meter maid of song
28. Genesis paradise
29. Rectangular paving stone
31. Barrett of early Pink Floyd

1	2	3	4	5		6	7	8	9	10
11						12				
13					14					
15								16		
			17				18			
19	20	21				22				
23					24					
25				26				27	28	29
30			31							
32						33				
34						35				

ANSWERS ON PAGE 189

NOTABLE NOVELISTS

ACROSS

1. Hoist with great effort
6. Abacus counters
11. Weird, in rap slang
12. Swashbuckling Flynn
13. Author of "The Snow Goose"
15. Like the Cheshire Cat
16. Four-wheeler, for short
17. "Evolve" artist DiFranco
18. Indonesian ox
19. Author of "The Prime of Miss Jean Brodie"
23. Elvis's middle name
24. Call ___ day
25. Bus. degree
26. Properly filed
30. Author of "The King Must Die"
32. Keep ___ to the ground (listen)
33. Bauer of clothing
34. Kind of slipper or maid
35. Appears (to be)

DOWN

1. "___ Don't Lie" (#1 song for Shakira)
2. Babylonia's ancient rival
3. His, in Paris
4. Baddie
5. It's under the hood
6. Its cap. is Brussels
7. Goethe's "The ___-King"
8. Pop star Grande
9. Medical school graduate
10. Czech neighbor
14. Dye in blue jeans
18. "I Love ___"
19. Moose or mouse
20. Fighting Illini campus site
21. Howled like a lion
22. Paving pieces
26. Factory seconds: abbr.
27. Guy, to a Valley Girl
28. Tournament format, briefly
29. AAA recommendations
31. "Hurrah!"

ANSWERS ON PAGE 189

SURPRISING SCIENTISTS

ACROSS

1. Gun that can stun
6. Scottish town
11. Basket-making fiber
12. Majorca for one
13. Dutch microscopist who discovered bacteria and blood cells and had no training in science
15. Teacup poodles, e.g.
16. 180 degrees from SSW
17. Energy unit
18. Eliot novel "Adam ___"
19. Persian mathematician who's better known for his Rubaiyat
23. Hounds for payment
24. CD followers?
25. Ron who played Tarzan
26. Party hearty
30. Austrian physicist known for a paradoxical cat
32. British unit of 14 pounds
33. Ma's instruments
34. Egypt's ___ Dam
35. Safe havens, old-style

DOWN

1. Cash register part
2. Boating on the briny
3. Ladder rung
4. Evasive ones
5. Try a new approach to
6. Places for corn or coal
7. Seat wedding guests, slangily
8. Mickey of "National Velvet"
9. Jackson with two Best Actress Oscars
10. Basketballer Olajuwon
14. Brainiac
18. Things best let be, proverbially
19. Forsyth's "The ___ File"
20. Swindles
21. "Notwithstanding that…"
22. Kenya's continent
26. "Fargo" filmmaker Joel or Ethan
27. Like a gargoyle

28. Unload, as stock

29. Suffix with ranch

31. Genetic matter, briefly

1	2	3	4	5		6	7	8	9	10
11						12				
13					14					
15								16		
			17				18			
19	20	21				22				
23					24					
25				26				27	28	29
30			31							
32						33				
34						35				

A LITTLE ALLITERATION

ACROSS

1. Winger or Messing
6. "Sully's" profession
11. Was broadcast
12. "J'Accuse" author Zola
13. Food product description that sounds like an oxymoron
15. Tetley tidbit
16. Half a Gabor sister
17. Prince Valiant's first son
18. Priory of ___: "The Da Vinci Code" secret society
19. What the adorable Southern belle had?
23. Sound measure
24. Old salt
25. Clod-busting tool
26. Dugout canoe
30. School cutups
32. Tyler of "The Talk"
33. Double-S arches
34. "The Highwayman" poet Alfred
35. Feel intuitively

DOWN

1. A little batty
2. Blarney Stone land
3. La ___ Tar Pits
4. Schedule again
5. Stick (to)
6. Stamp feature, in philately lingo
7. "If you ask me," in chatroom lingo
8. Tin ___: Model T
9. Nellie ___ (schoolmate of Laura Ingalls)
10. Room renter
14. Zealous devotee
18. Dickens miser
19. School of American art c. 1908
20. "Fantastic Voyage" rapper
21. Having the willies
22. Guitarist Santana
26. Some TV spots, briefly
27. Pop singer Stefani

28. French ones

29. "To be," to Caesar

31. Pronoun for a lady

1	2	3	4	5	■	6	7	8	9	10
11					■	12				
13					14					
15							■	16		
■			17			■	18			
19	20	21				22				
23				■	24			■		
25			■	26				27	28	29
30			31							
32					■	33				
34					■	35				

ANSWERS ON PAGE 190

ACROSS

1. Door, to Dante
6. Hatchery sounds
11. Menotti opera lad
12. Harpo Productions founder
13. Senate's locale
15. Proceeding as scheduled
16. Punk rock offshoot
17. It can mean "she," "you," or "they" in Germany
18. Blueprint detail, for short
19. Strawberry Fields locale
23. Commotions
24. Teachers' union: Abbr.
25. Society-page newcomer
26. Celebrity
30. The world's largest gorge
32. "I Still See ___" ("Paint Your Wagon" song)
33. Final purpose, to Aristotle
34. Put off for a while
35. Make blank

DOWN

1. Rabanne of fashion
2. Muscat is its capital
3. More than attentive
4. Needs water
5. Early hobbyist's computer
6. Eleventh president
7. NT book attributed to Paul
8. City down the shore from Buffalo, N.Y.
9. Golf great Arnold
10. Shoddy goods
14. Of the sea
18. Brit's wrench
19. Mooched
20. English Channel swimmer Gertrude
21. Prosecutor's request at a murder hearing
22. Papal envoy
26. Cake-and-candles time, briefly
27. "The Clan of the Cave Bear" heroine
28. Cattle calls

29. Massachusetts' motto start

31. Code-breaking org.

1	2	3	4	5		6	7	8	9	10
11						12				
13					14					
15								16		
			17				18			
19	20	21				22				
23					24					
25				26				27	28	29
30			31							
32						33				
34						35				

ANSWERS ON PAGE 190

BEFORE THEY WERE STARS

ACROSS

1. Owed money
5. Gear for bullfighters
10. Hi and bye on Lanai
12. Eyelike openings
13. Ilyena Lydia Vasilievna Mironov gained fame as...
15. Big Bad Wolf's demand
16. "So ___ heard!"
17. Cabinet dept. concerned with farming
18. Celebes ox
19. Frances Gumm is better known as...
23. Cat or clock preceder
24. "Volare (___ Blu Dipinto di Blu)"
25. Battleship inits.
26. Condenses on a surface
30. Eileen Regina Edwards? You'd call her...
32. Helped through difficulty (with "over")
33. Kind of blue suit
34. Ejects, as lava
35. Frankie Avalon hit "___ Dinah"

DOWN

1. "James and the Giant Peach" author
2. CSA Gen. Robert
3. Cloth bundle
4. Hold this
5. Dispute decider, at times
6. Crossword puzzler's dir.
7. Fancy Feast maker
8. Hinged flap on a plane's wing
9. Irish singer O'Connor
11. Lay ___ (bomb)
14. Prospero's daughter in "The Tempest"
18. Gave permission
19. Renaissance fair contests
20. Remove from the vessel
21. "Justine" author, the Marquis ___
22. Puts one's feet up
26. Gives a hand

27. Just barely cooked
28. Dallas nickname
29. Snick-or-___ (fight with knives)
31. Novel

1	2	3	4			5	6	7	8	9
10				11		12				
13					14					
15								16		
			17				18			
19	20	21				22				
23					24					
25				26				27	28	29
30			31							
32						33				
34							35			

ANSWERS ON PAGE 190

BUSTED!

ACROSS

1. Deep voices at the opera
6. Exemplary
11. Pianist Rubinstein
12. Porsche 911 model
13. Indian peace symbol
15. Spanish, in Spain
16. Vienna's country: abbr.
17. Gradually slowing, in mus.
18. "Tell ___ the marines!"
19. 1966 Hitchcock thriller
23. Spread for bread
24. Word of good cheer?
25. Sport drink suffix
26. Toronto's province
30. Blink of an eye
32. Lopez of "The Dirty Dozen"
33. "___ Macabre" (Saint-Saens work)
34. Sinatra's repertoire
35. Tiny biters

DOWN

1. Bunyan's Blue Ox
2. JFK landings
3. Red means this
4. First president of Indonesia
5. Promoting peace
6. Stressed type, for short
7. Patriotic women's org.
8. Book mistakes
9. Guinea pig's cousin
10. Food writer Nigella
14. Sign to continue straight
18. Resident of Cornell University's town
19. "Skoal" and "cheers"
20. Seasoned hand
21. Land, as a marlin
22. Kid-friendly, film-wise
26. Elevator inventor
27. TV tabloid pioneer Barrett
28. Hosp. or univ.
29. Shelley poems
31. Gerund suffix

ANSWERS ON PAGE 190

ON THE SCREEN OR IN NATURE

ACROSS

7. Coleslaw, often
8. Hopped a plane
9. Goldie Hawn flick or desert bloom
10. AARP member
12. "Forget about it!"
14. Journalist's basics
16. Bowling alley worker, once
17. Young people's drama of old
20. "___ me up, Scotty!"
21. Black gold

DOWN

1. "Wassup!"
2. Simple word processing format
3. California coastal region
4. Jill of "The Love Boat"
5. Hardly any
6. In the old days
11. Villain's exploit
13. Nautical danger
15. Give some lip to
16. Turn down
18. Sonogram area
19. Give off

ANSWERS ON PAGE 191

MERRY MEDLEY

ACROSS

1. Freight sent by plane
5. "Dinner's ready" sound
8. Europe, Asia and Africa
9. Bourbon Street side
11. Exhale with relief
14. Far and wide
15. Toy pistol
17. Blue footwear for Elvis
20. "Dream on!"
21. Clean with a broom
22. The Knickerbockers song about mendacity
23. "That's life!"

DOWN

1. A bad way to run
2. Ill-mannered
3. Financially viable
4. Cut to a roving reporter
6. Nuclear research city
7. Greet effusively
10. At-ease position for soldiers
12. Basic grading system
13. Something for nothing
16. "Tommy" band
18. Big name in clowning
19. Mayberry cell dweller

ANSWERS ON PAGE 191

ACROSS

4. Cross the threshold
5. "Amen!"
7. Former incarnation
9. Calcium source
10. Lions and tigers and bears
13. Cause trouble
15. Leave at the altar
16. Barking wanderer
18. Monk habitats
19. Clove hitch, for example

DOWN

1. Gold from the Magi, e.g.
2. Mail from a sweetheart
3. "You're blocking the view!"
4. Egg carton rating
6. Absorbent powder
8. "No way, Jose!"
11. Lab vessel
12. Gracefully step down
14. "Me, me, me" sort
17. Abrupt pull

ANSWERS ON PAGE 191

MIXED UP

ACROSS

1. Clicking site
5. Brother of Cain
8. Invitation exhortation
9. Day one
10. Shade providers on safari
12. Cool hangout
14. Confirm, as a password
16. "What do we have here?"
19. Deep distress
20. Red sky at morning, to a sailor
21. Cushy
22. "Let's get started!"

DOWN

1. "Flash" gatherings
2. "Gimme a highfive!"
3. When the voters choose
4. "Queen of Soul" Franklin
6. Incidentally
7. Dangerous place
9. "Tea for Two," for one
11. Signs of modesty on statues
13. Close hermetically
15. Beginner
17. "Home, James"
18. Data briefly

ANSWERS ON PAGE 191

LOTS OF B'S

ACROSS

1. Picnic drink holder
6. Fancy-schmancy
8. Film with a chariot race
9. Amusingly twisted
10. City of David
11. A bit bawdy
12. Tear dabber
14. Little traveled way
15. Mild stimulant from a palm tree
17. Exploded, with "up"
18. Business owner's goal
19. Having posted bond
20. Annoying kid
21. Announcement medium

DOWN

2. Mistake by the staff
3. "Hallelujah" Leonard
4. Place for a stud
5. Artful Dodger, for one
6. Chance for a shot
7. Vessel intended for combat
13. Stay in shape
14. Ballpark aides
16. Still asleep
17. How some students get to school

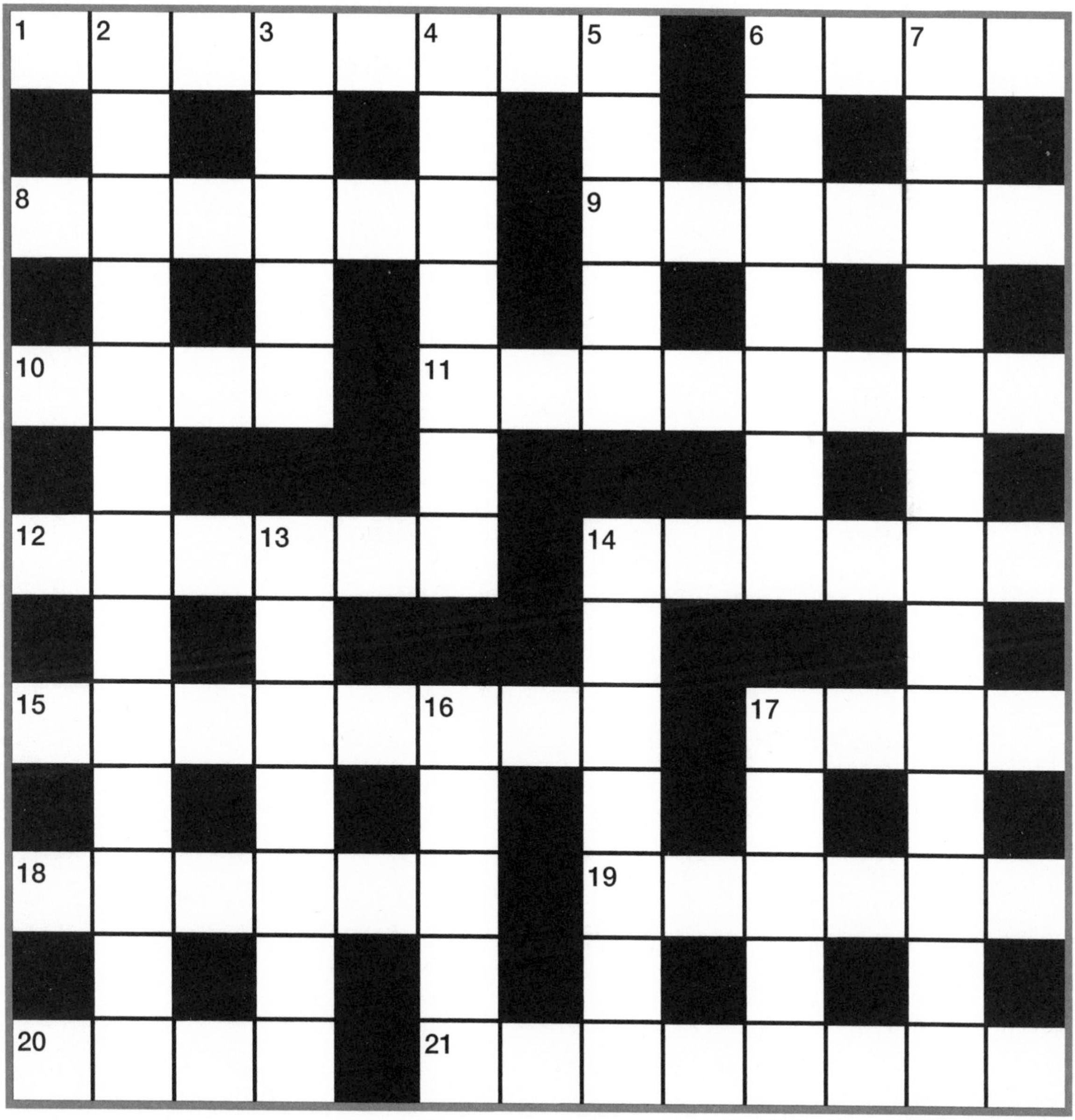

ANSWERS ON PAGE 192

AIR AND SPACE

ACROSS

5. Fruity cookie
7. Cups and saucers
9. "Battlestar Galactica" and such
10. Do a spit take, e.g.
11. Term of endearment
13. Completely rational
15. Adoring Biblical trio
17. Takes the plunge
19. Afraid to fire
20. Type of date on food packaging

DOWN

1. Closes, as a windbreaker
2. Nonworking hours
3. Brand of swabs
4. Handles the details of
6. Say what you saw in court
8. Where people get off of planes
12. Fried egg option
14. Eases off
16. "Great" fictional character
18. "Empire" actor Diggs

ANSWERS ON PAGE 192

CLUE STEW

ACROSS

1. Small power source
6. What to do after a shampoo
7. Sat for a photo
9. Go unhurriedly
10. Like some lunch orders
11. Accompany
13. Fast food burger
16. Capital of New Mexico
18. "Wheel of Fortune" buy
20. "Hound Dog" singer
21. Casino VIP
22. Places to pull off the highway

DOWN

1. Enola Gay payload
2. Creditor's loss
3. Holder of balls and dolls
4. American in Paris, e.g.
5. "Of course, dear lady"
6. Noble act
8. "Work beckons!"
12. Persuaded
14. Kind of fertilization
15. Dangles a carrot before
17. Altar recesses
19. Cabin location

ANSWERS ON PAGE 192

FOOD AND DRINK

ACROSS

1. Watches one's mouth?
5. Spit out
8. A crankshaft drives it
9. Clarifying exchange
10. Difficult situations
12. "Not so fast!"
14. Command to relax
16. Prohibitionists' target
19. Mo of Arizona politics
20. Be unfaithful to
21. "For Pete's ___!"
22. Candlelit spot, perhaps

DOWN

1. Brit's elevator
2. Beverage in a big bowl
3. Shocking fish
4. Duplication marks
6. Box opener of myth
7. "How you doin'?"
9. Single-beat symbol, often
11. Decathlon events in a circle
13. Recline
15. "Have a good day!" reply
17. American Indian corn
18. Shed a tear

ANSWERS ON PAGE 192

ANSWER KEY

Hodgepodge
(page 4)

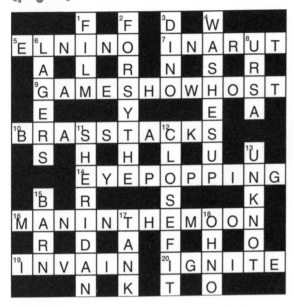

Grab Bag
(page 8)

Medley
(page 6)

A Bit of Wordplay
(page 10)

Common Phrases
(page 12)

An Ocular Puzzle
(page 14)

Potpourri
(page 16)

Phrase Assortment
(page 18)

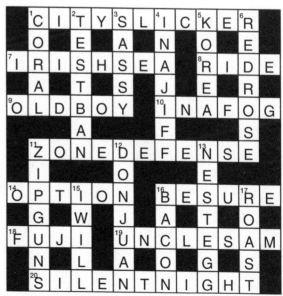

ANSWER KEY

Times and Places
(page 20)

Best Time for a Party
(page 24)

Figurative Places
(page 22)

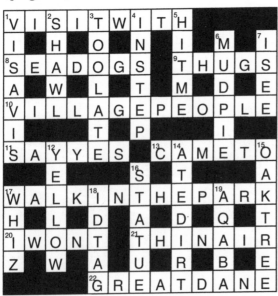

Written and Spoken
(page 26)

ANSWER KEY

Birds and Flowers
(page 28)

Red, White, Blue
(page 32)

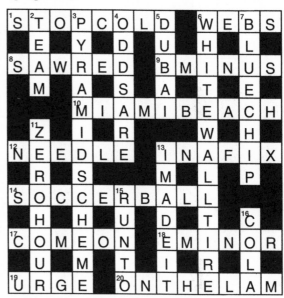

From Face to Feet
(page 30)

Knowledge Is Power
(page 34)

A Tasty Puzzle
(page 36)

Q Marks the Spot
(page 40)

Take a Chance
(page 38)

Fun and Games
(page 42)

It's in the Air
(page 44)

Melange
(page 48)

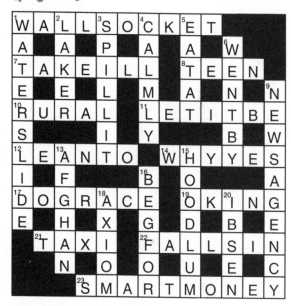

A Vacation from Cleaning
(page 46)

Three from ABC
(page 50)

ANSWER KEY

Across the Board
(page 52)

L	I	F	E		S	W	A	T	S
E	M	I	L		T	O	G	A	E
M	E	R	S		A	R	G	U	E
M	A	S	T	E	R	M	I	N	D
A	N	T	O	N		E	T	S	
		N	D	A	K				
I	S	P		P	I	M	A	S	
B	A	L	D	E	R	D	A	S	H
S	N	A	I	L		D	O	S	O
E	T	N	A	S		E	R	N	O
N	O	B	L	E		R	I	S	K

At the Drop of a Hat
(page 56)

K	E	P	I		A	L	A	N
A	R	O	N		S	A	G	A
R	A	B	E		A	C	A	D
S	T	O	V	E	P	I	P	E
T	O	Y	E	D		E	E	R
			R	U	G			
I	L	L		C	O	A	T	I
S	O	U	W	E	S	T	E	R
A	N	T	E		S	A	N	I
A	G	E	S		I	R	E	S
C	O	S	T		P	I	T	H

All in Good Time
(page 54)

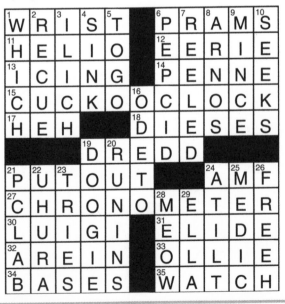

W	R	I	S	T		P	R	A	M	S
H	E	L	I	O		E	E	R	I	E
I	C	I	N	G		P	E	N	N	E
C	U	C	K	O	O	C	L	O	C	K
H	E	H			D	I	E	S	E	S
			D	R	E	D	D			
P	U	T	O	U	T		A	M	F	
C	H	R	O	N	O	M	E	T	E	R
L	U	I	G	I		E	L	I	D	E
A	R	E	I	N		O	L	L	I	E
B	A	S	E	S		W	A	T	C	H

At the Trattoria
(page 58)

E	D	S		B	A	S	E	S
R	I	A		O	C	E	A	N
A	N	T	I	P	A	S	T	O
S	E	E	M			T	S	R
			A	P	P	E	A	R
S	P	A	G	H	E	T	T	I
E	A	S	E	I	N			
A	M	I		T	A	P	A	
M	E	A	T	B	A	L	L	S
A	L	G	A	E		E	E	S
N	A	O	M	I		C	A	T

Best of Frenemies
(page 60)

M	A	R	C	S		A	L	I	B	I
B	L	O	O	M		H	A	N	E	S
A	B	O	M	I	N	A	T	I	O	N
S	A	M	P	L	E	S		T	N	T
		U	L	T		T	I	T	O	
C	A	P	T	A	I	N	H	O	O	K
A	F	O	E		Z	E	E			
S	G	T		S	E	E	M	S	T	O
T	H	E	M	A	N	D	A	R	I	N
L	A	N	A	S		L	L	A	N	O
E	N	T	R	E		E	L	S	E	S

Bye Now!
(page 64)

V	A	L	E			A	D	I	E	U
O	U	T	R	E		L	E	M	O	N
A	R	R	I	V	E	D	E	R	C	I
			V	A	C	A		E	E	S
S	U	M	A	C	H		C	A	N	Y
A	N	U	N		O	R	A	L	E	S
N	L	E		B	E	E	R			
D	O	S	V	I	D	A	N	I	Y	A
I	A	L	S	O		D	A	T	E	D
A	D	I	O	S			C	I	A	O

Body Talk
(page 62)

M	A	I	D		A	E	T	N	A
E	S	M	E		D	U	R	O	C
T	H	U	M	B	A	R	I	D	E
S	E	P	A	L		O	T	I	S
		N	I	T		I	C	I	
H	A	N	D	P	U	P	P	E	T
E	G	O		S	L	O			
L	O	B	S		I	L	I	A	C
M	O	U	T	H	P	I	E	C	E
E	S	T	A	R		T	S	A	R
T	E	S	T	S		E	T	R	E

Downward Dog
(page 66)

M	S	G	T		R	A	N	G	E	S
E	E	R	O		E	M	E	R	G	E
A	L	E	S		T	O	R	E	A	T
D	A	Y	C	A	R	E		A	D	S
			H	A	L	I	B	U	T	
S	N	O		B	E	A	R	D	E	D
P	A	U	L	I	V		B	A	T	E
C	A	N	I	N	E		A	N	T	S
A	N	D	S	O	R		N	E	U	E

ANSWER KEY

Dubious Definitions
(page 68)

B	I	O		N	A	A	C	P
A	R	R		O	S	L	E	R
D	E	C	O	M	P	O	S	E
E	S	A	U			T	A	M
		T	I	N	O	R	E	
D	E	B	R	I	E	F	E	D
A	R	R	E	S	T			
N	I	A		T	A	P	A	
D	E	S	E	R	V	I	N	G
E	P	S	O	N		D	I	E
R	A	Y	E	D		A	N	S

Grabbing Some Zs
(page 72)

Z	B	A	R		D	I	A	Z
A	L	D	A		A	R	N	E
P	I	Z	Z	A	P	I	E	S
S	N	E	E	R		S	S	T
			D	I	S			
A	L	L		S	T	A	G	G
Z	U	I	D	E	R	Z	E	E
I	T	N	O		A	A	R	E
Z	E	A	L		Y	N	E	Z

Fair Shares?
(page 70)

P	R	E	S	S		S	H	A
A	I	R	S	E	A		C	I	R
B	E	T	T	E	R	H	A	L	F
A	L	E	S		C	A	L	L	A
			E	A	S	I	E	R
S	E	C	O	N	D	H	A	L	F
T	R	E	N	D	Y	
E	R	L	E	S		C	A	N	E
F	O	L	D	I	N	H	A	L	F
F	R	A		T	H	E	A	R	T
I	S	R		A	R	A	B	S

Gripes of Wrath
(page 74)

G	I	R	D		J	O	K	E	D
I	S	A	O		O	N	E	N	O
L	I	N	O		E	E	R	I	E
A	N	G	R	Y	B	I	R	D	S
			S	I	L		I	S	T
G	A	O		N	O	T	
A	N	G	R	Y	W	O	R	D	S
S	I	D	E	A		S	E	E	A
U	T	E	N	N		A	N	A	T
P	A	N	D	G		Y	O	R	E

180

ANSWER KEY

Here and There
(page 76)

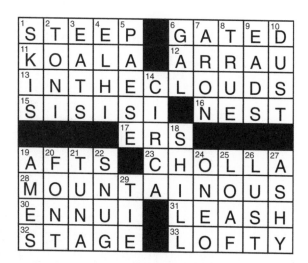

Across/grid answers:

P	A	D	R	E		T	A	P	A	S
C	L	O	U	D		I	L	O	N	A
P	I	C	T	U	R	E	T	H	I	S
S	T	S			A	T	O	L	L	S
			D	E	M	O	S			
P	A	R	O	L	E		C	D	S	
I	M	A	G	I	N	E	T	H	A	T
T	E	N	E	T		D	I	A	R	Y
A	N	I	S	E		A	N	N	E	X

High Time
(page 78)

S	T	E	E	P		G	A	T	E	D
K	O	A	L	A		A	R	R	A	U
I	N	T	H	E	C	L	O	U	D	S
S	I	S	I	S	I		N	E	S	T
			E	R	S				
A	F	T	S		C	H	O	L	L	A
M	O	U	N	T	A	I	N	O	U	S
E	N	N	U	I		L	E	A	S	H
S	T	A	G	E		L	O	F	T	Y

Inside Story
(page 80)

P	A	N	T		T	A	C	T
U	G	L	I		S	A	D	H	U
G	U	E	S	S	A	G	A	I	N
H	A	R	H	A	R		G	T	E
			R	N	A		I	O	R
D	E	P	I	C	T	I	O	N	S
A	N	I		T	O	M			
Y	A	N		I	G	E	T	I	T
S	M	A	R	T	A	L	E	C	S
P	O	T	S	Y		D	A	B	O
A	R	A	T		A	L	M	S

It's a Hit!
(page 82)

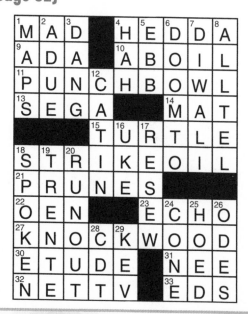

M	A	D		H	E	D	D	A
A	D	A		A	B	O	I	L
P	U	N	C	H	B	O	W	L
S	E	G	A		M	A	T
			T	U	R	T	L	E
S	T	R	I	K	E	O	I	L
P	R	U	N	E	S			
O	E	N		E	C	H	O
K	N	O	C	K	W	O	O	D
E	T	U	D	E		N	E	E
N	E	T	T	V		E	D	S

181

ANSWER KEY

Signs, Signs, Signs
(page 84)

A	B	A	R		D	O	H	A
P	O	P	E		E	N	E	R
P	H	E	N	O	M	E	N	A
L	O	R	A	X		C	R	I
		M	O	R	A	Y	S
S	O	M	E	N	E	R	V	E
C	U	E	S	I	N		
H	I	S		A	T	S	E	A
W	O	M	E	N	S	L	I	B
A	U	E	L		T	I	N	A
S	I	R	S		O	M	E	N

Switch It Up
(page 88)

P	A	W	S		S	A	C	K	S
O	R	I	N		A	L	A	N	A
P	I	S	A		D	E	N	O	M
S	A	C	R	E	D	C	O	W	S
			E	S	L		E	N	A
T	M	S		T	E	A		
S	A	C	R	E	D	V	O	W	S
A	G	R	E	E		A	R	E	A
R	E	A	L	M		S	C	A	N
S	E	G	O	S		T	A	R	S

Letter Change
(page 86)

E	L	M	S		S	C	O	P	E
D	O	E	S		I	M	P	E	L
A	G	R	E	A	T	D	E	A	L
M	O	E		L	O	R	D	L	Y
			P	I	N	S		
W	A	S	A	B	I		O	D	E
A	G	R	E	A	T	M	E	A	L
R	E	T	A	B		M	U	R	K
D	E	A	N	A		E	F	T	S

Altered Sequence
(page 90)

B	E	D		M	E	D	A	L	S
O	A	R		I	B	E	R	I	A
G	R	E	E	N	B	E	A	N	S
S	N	I	D	E			B	E	S
			U	R	D	U		
A	O	L		I	S	S	U	E
G	R	E	E	N	J	E	A	N	S
E	M	I	L	I	O		G	I	T
S	E	A	M	E	N		E	T	S

Go Together
(page 92)

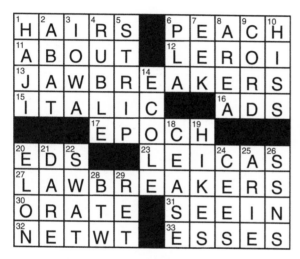

Making Waves
(page 96)

Another Letter Change
(page 94)

Name the Play
(page 98)

ANSWER KEY

Math Jokes
(page 100)

A	R	E	D		D	A	D	O
R	O	N	I		C	M	O	N
F	U	N	C	T	I	O	N	S
S	E	E	T	V		N	A	P
			U	G	A	R	T	E
F	O	R	M	U	L	A	I	C
T	H	E	S	I	S			
R	E	P		D	O	S	E	D
O	N	A	V	E	R	A	G	E
O	R	I	S			A	R	A	B
P	Y	R	O		N	A	N	S

Rhyme Time
(page 104)

B	E	A	M		S	T	R	I	P	E
O	L	D	E		L	A	U	R	E	L
S	K	I	N	N	Y	J	E	A	N	S
E	S	P	A	N	A			S	T	A
			T	E	S	L	A			
M	C	A		A	O	R	T	A	S	
F	U	L	L	O	F	B	E	A	N	S
A	L	B	I	N	O		A	D	E	N
S	P	A	C	E	X		S	A	W	S

Olé!
(page 102)

B	A	R	T		T	B	S	P
Y	E	A	H		W	O	O	L
T	O	T	E	M	P	O	L	E
E	N	A	M	I		B	E	A
		A	R	T	O	I	S	
T	I	T	L	E	R	O	L	E
I	M	E	L	D	A			
G	P	A		I	N	C	A	S
L	E	M	O	N	S	O	L	E
O	D	E	S		O	R	A	L
N	E	D	S		M	E	W	L

Riddles
(page 106)

L	O	M	B		A	P	B	S
I	T	S	Y		T	H	A	T
N	I	G	H	T	M	A	R	E
A	S	T	E	W		S	T	E
			A	E	G	E	A	N
S	P	A	R	E	R	I	B	S
W	A	N	T	T	O			
A	L	T		E	W	O	K	S
B	L	O	O	D	B	A	N	K
B	A	N	E		A	H	O	Y
Y	S	E	R		G	U	T	S

184

ANSWER KEY

Seuss for Youse
(page 108)

C	O	D	A		D	O	S	E	D
O	N	E	D		E	S	T	A	R
N	E	R	O		E	L	A	T	E
J	I	M	B	O	J	O	N	E	S
		E	R	A		D	R	S	
O	S	A		A	Y	N			
F	O	X	I	N	S	O	C	K	S
F	L	I	N	G		M	E	E	T
E	V	A	D	E		A	D	E	E
R	E	L	O	S		D	E	N	T

Temperature Rising
(page 112)

R	A	T	O	U	T		C	L	U
A	D	O	L	P	H		H	I	P
C	O	O	L	I	E	H	A	T	S
E	S	T	A		R	A	N	C	H
				L	A	N	D	H	O
W	A	R	M	U	P	S	U	I	T
I	D	I	O	C	Y				
G	R	A	D	Y		G	A	I	A
H	O	T	E	L	L	O	B	B	Y
T	I	A		I	A	G	R	E	E
S	T	S		U	B	O	A	T	S

Small Change
(page 110)

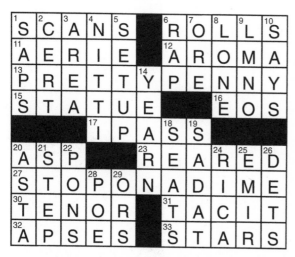

S	C	A	N	S		R	O	L	L	S
A	E	R	I	E		A	R	O	M	A
P	R	E	T	T	Y	P	E	N	N	Y
S	T	A	T	U	E		E	O	S	
			I	P	A	S	S			
A	S	P		R	E	A	R	E	D	
S	T	O	P	O	N	A	D	I	M	E
T	E	N	O	R		T	A	C	I	T
A	P	S	E	S		S	T	A	R	S

Quick Count
(page 114)

S	L	A	M	S		B	E	S	O	T
T	A	B	A	C		E	X	T	R	O
O	N	E	M	O	R	E	T	I	M	E
P	A	L	M	T	O	P		C	O	T
			O	C	T		O	K	L	A
T	W	O	T	H	U	M	B	S	U	P
R	A	S	H		N	A	E			
I	S	P		O	D	D	S	A	R	E
T	H	R	E	E	A	M	I	G	O	S
E	M	E	N	D		E	T	U	I	S
R	E	Y	E	S		N	Y	A	L	A

185

ANSWER KEY

Rhyme It
(page 116)

S	C	A	D	S		T	I	A	R	A
O	R	N	O	T		I	R	M	A	S
L	U	G	G	A	G	E	T	A	G	S
S	E	E	D	P	O	D		R	T	E
		A	L	G		G	N	A	T	
P	R	A	Y	E	R	F	L	A	G	S
L	E	T	S		E	R	A			
U	S	O		G	E	I	S	H	A	S
R	U	N	N	I	N	G	G	A	G	S
A	M	E	A	N		H	O	J	O	S
L	E	D	T	O		T	W	I	G	S

Things We Got from the Brits
(page 120)

A	L	A	R	M		A	T	L	A	S
C	A	R	E	T		R	H	I	N	E
T	H	E	C	O	M	P	U	T	E	R
A	R	A	L	S	E	A		C	M	A
		U	S	A		S	H	I	P	
T	H	E	S	A	N	D	W	I	C	H
H	O	N	E		S	U	E			
E	L	D		A	I	R	D	A	T	E
F	L	U	S	H	T	O	I	L	E	T
T	O	R	S	O		C	S	T	A	R
S	W	E	E	P		S	H	A	K	E

Terms of Art
(page 118)

H	A	R	S	H		M	A	M	A	S
A	L	O	H	A		O	P	A	R	T
F	E	T	E	G	A	L	A	N	T	E
T	R	O	I	L	U	S		C	H	R
		L	E	T		S	H	U	N	
C	H	I	A	R	O	S	C	U	R	O
O	O	N	S		C	U	R			
S	A	G		C	U	L	O	T	T	E
T	R	O	M	P	E	L	O	E	I	L
A	S	T	R	A		E	G	A	D	S
R	E	S	T	S		N	E	M	E	A

Three by King
(page 122)

C	O	M	M	A		A	L	E	R	T
I	S	A	I	D		D	I	R	E	R
T	H	E	D	E	A	D	Z	O	N	E
E	A	S	E	S	I	N		I	O	N
		A	T	L		A	C	I	D	
P	E	T	S	E	M	A	T	A	R	Y
R	N	O	T		E	L	L			
E	C	U		E	N	T	A	I	L	S
F	I	R	E	S	T	A	R	T	E	R
A	N	E	N	T		I	G	E	T	A
B	A	R	D	S		R	E	N	T	S

Six Authors
(page 124)

A	G	E	E		A	D	A	M	S
D	I	S	T		K	A	U	A	I
J	D	S	A	L	I	N	G	E	R
U	D	E		O	N	T			
R	A	N	B	Y		E	E	G	S
E	P	E	E		I	S	L	E	T
		S	B	A		A	N	O	
J	R	R	T	O	L	K	I	E	N
O	R	I	O	N		I	N	R	E
B	R	O	W	N		M	E	A	D

Fun on the High Seas
(page 128)

S	A	G	A		G	A	L	A	
L	I	A	R	S		I	M	I	N
A	D	I	E	T		R	A	N	D
W	A	T	E	R	S	L	I	D	E
		L	A	T		D	A	S	
E	R	A		N	A	M			
C	O	M	E	D	Y	A	C	T	S
O	B	E	Y		A	D	O	R	E
L	I	N	E		T	A	K	E	A
E	N	D	S		M	E	E	T	

Summer Fun
(page 126)

G	A	M	E		S	H	E	L	L
O	V	E	N		T	E	D	D	Y
S	A	N	D	C	A	S	T	L	E
S	T	A		B	R	O			
I	A	G	O	S		U	S	M	A
P	R	E	S		O	T	T	E	R
	T	O	T		U	A	R		
W	A	T	E	R	S	E	D	G	E
A	C	R	A	B		D	I	E	S
S	A	I	L	S		S	O	R	T

Comfort Food
(page 130)

S	M	A	L	L		E	L	M	S
H	A	N	O	I		P	E	A	L
A	M	I	G	O		E	T	N	A
H	A	M	A	N	D	E	G	G	S
	N	C	O		O	O	H		
A	P	A		U	G	H			
H	A	S	H	B	R	O	W	N	S
E	L	S	A		A	N	A	I	L
M	E	E	T		C	O	S	M	O
S	O	T	S		E	R	A	S	E

Bouncing Back
(page 132)

Across/grid answers: BISTRO, AKIN, UNCORK, TAME, SARTRE, ARIE, KNEE, ERRAND, SEE, ACEIT, CATHY, ESP, MAHALO, ECHO, YEOH, BATHOS, ORWE, EXTORT, BOLD, ELOPES

Doohickeys
(page 136)

MOAB, CARAT, ABIE, PANAMA, CONTRAPTION, ELUSIVE, LRG, ONE, EAL, WHANGDOODLE, EEG, RVS, NEL, TOUCANS, THINGAMAJIG, AENEID, RANT, SETOF, SRAS

Cities in Song
(page 134)

CABLE, AWACS, ILIAL, DIDAH, GARYINDIANA, SILICON, GIS, NIT, PINT, CHATTANOOGA, OENO, TOR, MCA, TENTPEG, BAKERSFIELD, ATIDE, ACELA, TENDS, TOPSY

Eco-friendly
(page 138)

GEMS, RAIDS, ELIM, DECREE, NATALIECOLE, AMTRAC, NAS, TSK, TINA, ELSIETHECOW, NATE, REA, RAR, ARPELS, ALICECOOPER, PAPACY, TENT, TAEBO, SETA

America
(page 140)

A	V	A	S	T		R	E	A	D	S
D	I	N	A	H		N	E	M	E	A
A	T	I	M	E	T	O	K	I	L	L
S	O	L	O	I	S	T		N	A	L
			S	S	H		T	O	N	O
S	Y	C	A	M	O	R	E	R	O	W
T	O	E	S		M	O	A			
I	O	R		O	B	S	C	U	R	E
T	H	E	B	R	E	T	H	R	E	N
C	O	A	S	T		E	M	E	N	D
H	O	L	E	S		R	E	S	T	S

Notable Novelists
(page 144)

H	E	A	V	E		B	E	A	D	S
I	L	L	I	N		E	R	R	O	L
P	A	U	L	G	A	L	L	I	C	O
S	M	I	L	I	N	G		A	T	V
		A	N	I		A	N	O	A	
M	U	R	I	E	L	S	P	A	R	K
A	R	O	N		I	T	A			
M	B	A		I	N	O	R	D	E	R
M	A	R	Y	R	E	N	A	U	L	T
A	N	E	A	R		E	D	D	I	E
L	A	D	Y	S		S	E	E	M	S

You Know My Name
(page 142)

S	A	L	E	M		M	E	S	A	S
L	L	A	N	O		A	R	T	S	Y
I	T	S	T	W	O	G	R	O	S	S
M	O	S	A	I	C	S		P	U	T
		I	N	T		P	A	C	E	
A	N	A	L	G	O	R	I	T	H	M
G	A	R	S		M	E	N			
A	S	L		C	O	H	E	R	E	S
T	H	E	S	A	M	E	S	I	D	E
H	U	E	Y	S		M	O	T	E	T
A	A	N	D	E		S	L	A	N	T

Surprising Scientists
(page 146)

T	A	S	E	R		B	U	R	G	H
I	S	T	L	E		I	S	O	L	A
L	E	E	U	W	E	N	H	O	E	K
L	A	P	D	O	G	S		N	N	E
		E	R	G		B	E	D	E	
O	M	A	R	K	H	A	Y	Y	A	M
D	U	N	S		E	F	G			
E	L	Y		C	A	R	O	U	S	E
S	C	H	R	O	D	I	N	G	E	R
S	T	O	N	E		C	E	L	L	I
A	S	W	A	N		A	S	Y	L	A

ANSWER KEY

A Little Alliteration
(page 148)

D	E	B	R	A		P	I	L	O	T
A	I	R	E	D		E	M	I	L	E
F	R	E	S	H	F	R	O	Z	E	N
T	E	A	L	E	A	F		Z	S	A
		A	R	N		S	I	O	N	
A	C	U	T	E	A	C	C	E	N	T
S	O	N	E		T	A	R			
H	O	E		P	I	R	O	G	U	E
C	L	A	S	S	C	L	O	W	N	S
A	I	S	H	A		O	G	E	E	S
N	O	Y	E	S		S	E	N	S	E

American Landmarks
(page 150)

P	O	R	T	A		P	E	E	P	S
A	M	A	H	L		O	P	R	A	H
C	A	P	I	T	O	L	H	I	L	L
O	N	T	R	A	C	K		E	M	O
		S	I	E		S	P	E	C	
C	E	N	T	R	A	L	P	A	R	K
A	D	O	S		N	E	A			
D	E	B		B	I	G	N	A	M	E
G	R	A	N	D	C	A	N	Y	O	N
E	L	I	S	A		T	E	L	O	S
D	E	L	A	Y		E	R	A	S	E

Before They Were Stars
(page 152)

D	E	B	T		C	A	P	E	S	
A	L	O	H	A		O	C	U	L	I
H	E	L	E	N	M	I	R	R	E	N
L	E	T	M	E	I	N		I	V	E
			A	G	R		A	N	O	A
J	U	D	Y	G	A	R	L	A	N	D
O	N	E	O		N	E	L			
U	S	S		A	D	S	O	R	B	S
S	H	A	N	I	A	T	W	A	I	N
T	I	D	E	D		S	E	R	G	E
S	P	E	W	S		D	E	D	E	

Busted!
(page 154)

B	A	S	S	I		I	D	E	A	L
A	R	T	U	R		T	A	R	G	A
B	R	O	K	E	N	A	R	R	O	W
E	S	P	A	N	O	L		A	U	S
			R	I	T		I	T	T	O
T	O	R	N	C	U	R	T	A	I	N
O	L	E	O		R	A	H			
A	D	E		O	N	T	A	R	I	O
S	P	L	I	T	S	E	C	O	N	D
T	R	I	N	I		D	A	N	S	E
S	O	N	G	S		G	N	A	T	S

ANSWER KEY

On the Screen or in Nature
(page 156)

■	1H	■	2T	■	3B	■	4W	■	5A	■	6Y	■
7S	I	D	E	D	I	S	H	■	8F	L	E	W
■	Y	■	X	■	G	■	E	■	E	■	A	■
9C	A	C	T	U	S	F	L	O	W	E	R	■
■	■	■	F	■	U	■	A	■	■	■	S	■
10S	11E	N	I	O	R	■	12N	O	13S	O	A	P
■	V	■	L	■	■	■	■	■	A	■	G	■
14F	I	V	E	W	15S	■	16P	I	N	B	O	Y
■	L	■	■	■	M	■	A	■	D	■	■	■
■	17D	A	18W	S	O	N	S	C	R	E	19E	K
■	E	■	O	■	O	■	S	■	E	■	M	■
20B	E	A	M	■	21C	R	U	D	E	O	I	L
■	D	■	B	■	H	■	P	■	F	■	T	■

In the Wild
(page 160)

■	■	■	1G	■	■	■	2L	■	3L	■	■	■
■	4G	O	I	N	■	5S	O	B	E	I	6T	■
■	R	■	F	■	■	■	V	■	T	■	A	■
7P	A	S	T	L	8I	F	E	■	9M	I	L	K
■	D	■	■	■	N	■	L	■	E	■	C	■
10M	E	A	11T	E	A	T	E	R	S	■	■	■
■	A	■	E	■	P	■	T	■	E	■	12B	■
■	■	■	13S	T	I	R	T	H	E	P	O	T
■	14D	■	T	■	G	■	E	■	■	■	W	■
15J	I	L	T	■	16S	T	R	A	17Y	D	O	G
■	V	■	U	■	E	■	■	■	A	■	U	■
■	18A	B	B	E	Y	S	■	19K	N	O	T	■
■	■	■	E	■	E	■	■	■	K	■	■	■

Merry Medley
(page 158)

1A	I	2R	C	3A	R	4G	O	■	5G	6O	N	7G
M	■	U	■	B	■	O	■	■	■	A	■	L
8O	L	D	W	O	R	L	D	■	9O	K	R	A
K	■	E	■	V	■	I	■	10P	■	R	■	D
■	■	■	11H	E	A	V	E	A	S	I	G	H
12P	■	13F	■	W	■	E	■	R	■	D	■	A
14A	B	R	O	A	D	■	15C	A	P	G	U	N
S	■	E	■	T	■	16T	■	D	■	E	■	D
17S	U	E	D	E	S	H	O	E	S	■	■	■
F	■	R	■	R	■	E	■	R	■	18B	■	19O
20A	S	I	F	■	21S	W	E	E	P	O	U	T
I	■	D	■	■	■	H	■	S	■	Z	■	I
22L	I	E	S	■	23S	O	I	T	G	O	E	S

Mixed Up
(page 162)

1M	O	2U	S	3E	P	4A	D	■	5A	6B	E	7L
O	■	P	■	L	■	R	■	■	■	Y	■	I
8B	E	T	H	E	R	E	■	9G	E	T	G	O
S	■	O	■	C	■	T	■	O	■	H	■	N
■	■	10P	I	T	H	H	E	L	M	E	T	S
11F	■	■	■	I	■	A	■	D	■	B	■	D
12I	N	13S	P	O	T	■	14R	E	T	Y	P	E
G	■	E	■	N	■	15N	■	N	■	■	■	N
16L	O	A	N	D	B	E	H	O	L	17D	■	■
E	■	L	■	A	■	W	■	L	■	R	■	18I
19A	G	O	N	Y	■	20B	A	D	S	I	G	N
F	■	F	■	■	■	I	■	I	■	V	■	F
21S	O	F	T	■	22H	E	R	E	W	E	G	O

ANSWER KEY

Lots of B's
(page 164)

Clue Stew
(page 168)

Air and Space
(page 166)

Food and Drink
(page 170)